SPANISH CHATBOOK

2

chat•book (*chat-bŭk*) —*noun*
1 : Our second-level conversational workbook with both present and past tense Spanish lessons and activities

BY

JULIE JAHDE POSPISHIL

SpanishChatCompany.com

Omaha, Nebraska

Revised Edition: June 2017

Copyright © 2013 by Spanish Chat Company

All rights reserved. No part of this book may be reproduced or transmitted in any form or by any means, electronic or mechanical, including photocopying, recording, or by any information storage and retrieval system, without permission in writing from the publisher.
The author acknowledges that there are many differences in language translation and have attempted to select a form of Spanish that will be understood in the vast majority of Spanish-speaking situations. For more information and to contact the authors: SpanishChatCompany.com.

ISBN 13: 978-0-9824625-8-4

ISBN 10: 0-9824625-8-1

LCCN: 2013917470

Library of Congress Cataloging-in Publication Data on file with publisher.

Published by: Spanish Chat Company
    SpanishChatCompany.com

SU TAREA = YOUR HOMEWORK

We will use this page to record our homework.

Homework will be checked at the beginning of each class.

PÁGINAS = PAGES	FIRME AQUÍ O PONGA PEGATINES = SIGN HERE OR PUT ON STICKERS
From Lesson 1 Pages 17 & 18 **DUE** _____	
From Lesson 2 Pages 27 & 28 **DUE** _____	
From Lesson 3 Pages 37 & 38 **DUE** _____	
From Lesson 4 Pages 47 & 48 **DUE** _____	
From Lesson 5 Pages 57 & 5 **DUE** _____	
From Lesson 6 Pages 67 & 68 **DUE** _____	
ROUGH DRAFT DUE _____	
FINAL PROJECT DUE _____	

THE SPANISH CHATBOOK AND SPANISH CHATBOOK 2 ARE HIGHLY RECOMMENDED TO LEARN SPANISH TODAY FOR WORK & PLAY:

I highly recommend the *Spanish Chatbook* activities which combine lessons on language, history and culture, all wrapped up in an energetic, dynamic presentation. As a principal at a Dual Language school, I have found the *Spanish Chatbook* classes have helped me communicate more effectively with my students and families. The *Spanish Chatbooks* make learning Spanish interesting, engaging and fun!

**Marjorie Schmid, Principal,
Crestridge Elementary International Studies &
Dual Language Magnet Center**

"Wow who would have thought that you could teach an old dog new tricks. What a great way to learn Spanish. Thank You"

Lonnie Conley, Elementary Paraprofessional

"*Spanish Chatbooks* are excellent books for learning the Spanish language in a classroom setting or individual study. The books contain charts of verb conjugation, pronunciation guides and fun activities. Cultural information included in the books is great for understanding Spanish-speaking people. An Answer Key is provided at the back of each book for checking yourself and giving immediate feedback. I recommend *Spanish Chatbook and Spanish Chatbook 2* for anyone wanting to learn the Spanish language."

Dona Zrust, elementary teacher

"*Spanish Chatbook* teaching methods are engaging and fun."

**Robin Jefferson,
OPS Head Start Administrative Assistant**

In our constantly changing multi-cultural society, it is becoming more necessary to learn a second language and expand our communication abilities. *Spanish Chatbooks* make this learning process fun and easy. I looked forward to attending classes each week and I learned so much. I cannot wait for classes to begin again. I use what I have learned in my daily communication with Spanish-speaking children & families. Muchas Gracias.

**Lyris R. Crowdy Peak, CSW, MSHS /LADC Intern
Governance & Parent Facilitator, OPS Head Start
Administration**

HERE IS WHAT PEOPLE ARE SAYING ABOUT OUR SPANISH CHATBOOK:

"This was the best Spanish learning experience I ever had. The class was extremely upbeat and fun. I will continue using her guides as a reference. Thanks!"

—**Tess Snyder
Woodmen of the World Insurance Agency**

"As a Training Manager for a regional casino, having our Leaders understand basic conversational Spanish is critical to their success in interacting with their teams. Julie does a phenomenal job making the classes she teaches fun and interactive. I would highly recommend Julie as a competent, passionate, and enthusiastic trainer."

—**Jackie Hansen, Casino Training Manager**

"As a tenured educator and facilitator I truly appreciated Julie's ability to flexibly adapt to multiple learning styles in her training/classroom. She infuses many aspects into her curriculum, hence maximizing student results. Two years of studying Spanish was nothing compared to what I learned in two weeks time with Julie. Her philosophy works!"

—**Spencer K. Terry, Private Consultant**

"When learning to speak a new language, students often feel shy or intimidated when trying to put together more than a few words. Spanish Chat Company's method of teaching Spanish makes the learning process fun and easy, so students show more confidence in pronouncing words and forming sentences. I would recommend these beneficial key words and phrases — whether for personal or business use."

—**Deb Barelos, Circulation Manager
Omaha Public Library**

"Spanish Chatbook with Maestra Julia is an experience of enthusiasm for the topic. She is pragmatic, able to teach at the appropriate level and yet challenging in a polite way."

—**Dr. Charles Filipi, Professor of Surgery
Creighton University**

ABOUT THE AUTHOR

Julie Jahde Pospishil studied for a semester at the University in San Sebastian, Spain, and has an M.A. in Education-Language Acquisition from the University of Nebraska–Omaha. She has taught Spanish for 18 years customizing Adult Spanish Classes for Omaha Public Schools, Boystown Pediatrics–Bergan Mercy Hospital, Omaha Public Power District (OPPD), Omaha Public Libraries, Dana College, Woodmen of the World, Casinos, Communications Companies, First Data Resources, many banks and Metropolitan Community College. She and her husband Brad own Spanish Chat Company, and love traveling together. They have spent time in 15 different Latin American countries, meeting many amigos. Julie currently teaches *Spanish Chatbook, Spanish Chatbook 2, Business Spanish Chatbook, Elementary Spanish Chatbook and Culinary Spanish Chatbook* classes. Julie produced an audio CD for Latina breast cancer survivors called, *"Un Tiempo para Sanar."* Julie enjoys cooking Latin American dishes with her children, Jaden and Elena. She believes "everyone smiles in the same language" and "donde existe voluntad, siempre hay un camino." = "Where there's a will, there's a way."

Contributor Brad Pospishil has been a Spanish teacher for the past 14 years at Omaha North Magnet High School. He has a B.A. from Rockhurst University and an M.S. from the University of Wisconsin–Madison in Industrial Relations. He studied Spanish at the University of Nebraska–Lincoln and at ITESM-Querétaro, México. He received his teaching certificate from UNL with endorsements in Spanish, history and government. Brad has traveled extensively in Latin America with his wife, Julie, on "Aventuras con Julia."

PRAISE FOR ANOTHER GREAT BOOK BUSINESS SPANISH CHATBOOK:

"The practical and enjoyable lessons were designed to teach our employees to communicate with our Spanish-speaking customers. We learned the language, plus important cultural facts about Spanish-speaking countries."

—Pat Tooles, Corporate Performance
Omaha Public Power District

"I have really enjoyed the *Business Spanish Chatbook*. The pronunciation guides and phrases are valuable tools that I use often in my day-to-day work."

—Jill Regester, Communications Manager
Woodmen of the World Insurance Agency

"The lessons are easy to follow and understand, and the phrases we learned were exactly what we needed to better serve our customers. Julie has that rare gift of making learning fun. She brings such exuberance to her classes, the students learn very easily."

—Terry Wingate, Volunteer Coordinator
Omaha Public Library

"I enjoyed the practical Spanish classes which were geared to the needs of our customer service department at OPPD."

—Joy Mota, Customer Service Center

ELEMENTARY SPANISH CHATBOOK IS GREAT FOR ELEMENTARY KIDS:

"It's just so much fun!! It is awesome! We get to make fun art and try new foods!"

—Connor, 4th grade

"The *Elementary Spanish Chatbook* activities have made Spanish learning fun for my daughter! She is able to teach the children not just the language, but much about the different Spanish cultures as well!"

—Maria Michaelis, M.D.
Mother of Elementary Spanish Student

OUR CULINARY SPANISH CHATBOOK IS ALSO GETTING RAVE REVIEWS:

"Welcome to the way you will learn Spanish. This is the perspective that should be taken with all languages. Gracias Maestra!"

—Phil Nicols, Culinary student

"Maestra Julia is an engaged and dynamic instructor in the classroom whose passion para el Español y la cocina has also permeated this project."

—Chef Brian O'Malley Academic Director
Institute for the Culinary Arts
Metropolitan Community College

"Culinary Spanish Chatbook is a 'must have' for everyone working in the food industry. There is nothing more frustrating than not being able to communicate with a co-worker. This book is a great tool to help break down those barriers, and it's realistic, upbeat approach makes learning Spanish fun."

—Karen Popp, Operations Manager
WheatFields Eatery and Bakery

Julie has taught Spanish for the Institute for the Culinary Arts for many years, and always to rave reviews from her students."

—James E. (Jim) Trebbien, Executive Director / Dean
Institute for the Culinary Arts

"Using this book to learn Spanish is a great way to show respect to people that you work with."

—Brian Isaacs, Executive Chef

INTRODUCTION: A TOUR OF THE BOOK

Welcome! = ¡Bienvenidos!

We are so glad you have joined this learning adventure, and we hope you will be able to use these phrases immediately. This book has useful, practical phrases designed to help anyone communicate with Hispanic friends and clients. We highly recommend using our *Spanish Chatbook* before this book as a first step on your Spanish journey and then using this *Spanish Chatbook 2*. If you are ready to go to the next level of communication, then this is the book for you.

Each lesson will take about 2-3 hours to complete. Each of the six lessons includes four verbs and many conversational phrases. Each lesson contains the group "controlled conversations," using four key verbs in many phrases, spoken practice activities, grammar tidbits, translation practice homework, flashcards, games and puzzles. Awareness of the Hispanic culture is woven into each lesson with facts about each Spanish-speaking country, trivia questions, and an explanation of cultural differences in styles with overall cultural diversity topics and considerations. For the activities, you will need dice, scissors and "Bingo" pieces made of small scraps of paper. A few partner exercises are included in each lesson. We recommend finding a friend, family member or native speaker to help you with some of these activities. A lunch study group that meets for an hour or two each week is ideal.

EL VOCABULARIO = THE VOCABULARY

LOS MESES DEL AÑO = THE MONTHS OF THE YEAR

- **enero** = January
- **febrero** = February
- **marzo** = March
- **abril** = April
- **mayo** = May
- **junio** = June
- **julio** = July
- **agosto** = August
- **septiembre** = September
- **octubre** = October
- **noviembre** = November
- **diciembre** = December

LOS DÍAS DE LA SEMANA = THE DAYS OF THE WEEK

- **domingo** = Sunday
- **lunes** = Monday
- **martes** = Tuesday
- **miércoles** = Wednesday
- **jueves** = Thursday
- **viernes** = Friday
- **sábado** = Saturday

EL CLIMA = THE WEATHER

- **Hace viento.** = It's windy.
- **Hace calor.** = It's hot.
- **Hace sol.** = It's sunny.
- **Hace frío y nieva.** = It's cold and snow.
- **Llueve.** = Rain
- **Está nublado.** = It's cloudy.

EL ALFABETO = THE ALPHABET

A	*ah*
B	*beh*
C	*seh*
D	*deh*
E	*eh*
F	*ehf-feh*
G	*heh*
H	*ah-cheh*
I	*eee* OR *(eee Latina)* *(Latina literally means the Latin Eee)*
J	*hoh-tah*
K	*kah*
L	*ehl-leh*
M	*ehm-meh*
N	*ehn-neh*
Ñ	*ehn-ñyeh*
O	*oh*
P	*peh*
Q	*koo*
R	*air-reh*
S	*ehs-seh*
T	*teh*
U	*oo*
V	*veh* OR *(oo-veh)*
W	*doh-bleh-veh* OR *(doh-bleh-oo)* *(In Spain = oo-veh doh-bleh)*
X	*eh-kees*
Y	*yeh* OR *(ee-gree-eh-gah)* *(Griega literally means the Greek Eee)*
Z	*seh-tah*

SPANISH CHATBOOK 2

INTRODUCCIÓN
1 UNO

INTRODUCTION / TABLE OF CONTENTS 1
   Queridos Estudiantes = Dear students: Notes about *Spanish Chatbook 2* 4
   Queridos Maestros = Dear teachers: Supplies needed and list of verbs for each lesson 5
   Frases Positivas = Positive phrases 6
   Audio = Audio: CD track listing 7
   Nombres = Names: A list of Spanish names / Name tag 8
   Mapa y Números = Map: Spanish-speaking countries & Numbers 1-100 9

LESSON 1: ¿LISTOS PARA CHARLAR? = READY TO CHAT?
   Empieza aquí = Start here: Spanish vowels and present tense **-ar** verbs 10
   Con sus compañeros = With your colleagues: A review of time 11
   Yo sé los verbos = I know the verbs: Present tense **-ar** verbs/ Flashcards 12
   Juego de "Tres en Raya = Three-in-a-row" game (Tic-Tac-Toe) 13
   Gramática = Grammar: Nouns, Definite and Indefinite Articles 14
   Cultura = Culture: Places to visit and Holidays in Spain 15
   Temas para conversar = Conversational topics 16
   Tarea = Homework: Translate the phrases 17
   Más tarea = More homework: **Crucigrama** = Crossword puzzle 18
   Ayúdame = Help me: A bonus game to practice verb conjugation 19

LESSON 2: ES LA HORA DE CHARLAR = IT IS TIME TO CHAT
   Empieza aquí = Start here: Present tense **-er and -ir** verbs (Tourist game) 20
   Con sus compañeros = With your colleagues: A conversational partner activity 21
   Yo sé los verbos = I know the verbs: Present tense **-er and -ir** verbs / Flashcards 22
   Juego de "Toma Todo = Take everything" game 23
   Gramática = Grammar: Affirmative and Negative 24
   Cultura = Culture: Places to visit and Holidays in Mexico 25
   Temas para conversar = Conversational topics 26
   Tarea = Homework: Translate the phrases 27
   Más tarea = More homework: **Buscapalabras** = Word search 28
   Ayúdame = Help me: A list of the -go -go verbs 29

LESSON 3: MÁS POR FAVOR = MORE PLEASE
   Empieza aquí = Start here: Present tense **-rulebreaker** verbs 30
   Con sus compañeros = With your colleagues: A conversational partner activity 31
   Yo sé los verbos = I know the verbs: Present tense **-rulebreaker** verbs / Flashcards 32
   Juego de "Alrededor del Mundo = Around the World" game & Final Project ideas 33
   Gramática = Grammar: Possessive adjectives and Possessive pronouns 34
   Cultura = Culture: Places to visit and Holidays in Central America 35
   Temas para conversar = Conversational topics 36
   Tarea = Homework: Translate and match the phrases 37
   Más tarea = More homework: **Adivinanza** = Guess the secret words puzzle 38
   Ayúdame = Help me: Lesson 1-3 present tense verbs chart / Interview and/or exam 39

INTRODUCCIÓN 2 DOS

SPANISH CHATBOOK 2

LESSON 4: SIGUE CHARLANDO = KEEP CHATTING

- **Empieza aquí** = Start here: Preterite and imperfect past tense -**ar** verbs 40
- **Con sus compañeros** = With your colleagues: A conversational partner activity 41
- **Yo sé los verbos** = I know the verbs: Past tense -**ar** verbs / Flashcards 42
- **Juego de "Verbos y Dados** = Verbs and Dice" game 43
- **Gramática** = Grammar: Demonstrative Adjectives and Pronouns 44
- **Cultura** = Culture: Bolivia, Colombia, Ecuador, Venezuela and Peru 45
- **Temas para conversar** = Conversational topics to create your own role play 46
- **Tarea** = Homework: Translate the phrases 47
- **Más tarea** = More homework: **Crucigrama** = Crossword puzzle 48
- **Ayúdame** = Help me: A chart of when to use preterite vs. imperfect 49

LESSON 5: CHARLAMOS UNA VEZ MÁS = LET'S CHAT ONE MORE TIME

- **Empieza aquí** = Start here: Preterite and imperfect past tense -**er** /-**ir** verbs 50
- **Con sus compañeros** = With your colleagues: A conversational partner activity 51
- **Yo sé los verbos** = I know the verbs: Past tense -**er** / -**ir** verbs / Flashcards 52
- **Juego de "Parejas"** = Game of "Pairs" a flashcard matching game 53
- **Gramática** = Grammar: Descriptive and Comparative Adjectives 54
- **Cultura** = Culture: Chile, Argentina, Uruguay and Paraguay 55
- **Temas para conversar** = Conversational topics 56
- **Tarea** = Homework: Translate the phrases 57
- **Más tarea** = More homework: **Buscapalabras** =Word search 58
- **Ayúdame** = Help me: A Final project Rubric 59

LESSON 6: TERMINAMOS CHARLANDO = WE FINISHED CHATTING

- **Empieza aquí** = Start here: Preterite and imperfect past tense **rule breaker** verbs 60
- **Con sus compañeros** = With your colleagues: a conversational partner activity 61
- **Yo sé los verbos** = I know the verbs: Past tense **rule breaker** verbs/ Flashcards 62
- **Juego de "Lotería"** = Game of "Bingo" 63
- **Gramática** = Grammar: Prepositions 64
- **Cultura** = Culture: Puerto Rico, Dominican Republic, Cuba and Equatorial Guinea 65
- **Temas** = **Topics**: Chart of the Preterite & Imperfect past tense verbs used in Lessons 4-6 66
- **Tarea** = Homework: Translate the phrases 67
- **Más tarea** = More homework: **Adivinanza** = Guess the secret word puzzle 68
- **Ayúdame** = Help me: 10 ideas to continue learning 69

SPANISH CHATBOOK 2

INTRODUCCIÓN 3 TRES

SU OPINIÓN = YOUR OPINION A Feedback Form

CERTIFICADO = CERTIFICATE A Certificate of Completion

APÉNDICE = APPENDIX
- **Recetas** = Recipes..70
- **Días Festivos** = Holidays 73
- Extra Grammar: Accent marks...76
- Extra Grammar: Gustar..78
- Extra Grammar: Indirect/direct object pronouns..79
- Extra Grammar: Reflexive / Present progressive..80
- Extra Grammar: Present tense -**ar**/-**er**/-**ir** verb conjugation. 81
- Extra Grammar: Boot verbs / Irregular present tense..83
- Extra Grammar: Irregular present tense..85
- Extra Grammar: Regular preterite past tense..86
- Extra Grammar: Irregular preterite past tense...87
- Extra Grammar: Irregular preterite past tense / Skateboard verbs...............................91
- Extra Grammar: Imperfect past tense..92
- Extra Grammar: Imperfect past tense verb conjugation / Irregular imperfect.............93
- Extra Grammar: Preterite vs. Imperfect..94
- **English** = **Spanish** Glossary of vocabulary...95
- **Español** = **Inglés** Glosario de vocabulario 105
- **60 Verbos** = 60 verbs in present, preterite & imperfect tenses.................................114

LAS RESPUESTAS = THE ANSWERS An Answer Key for Lessons 1–6 & Extra Grammar

ÍNDICE = INDEX

GRACIAS = THANK YOU

¿NECESITA ALGO MÁS? = DO YOU NEED ANYTHING ELSE? An Order Form for:
*Spanish Chatbook, Culinary Spanish Chatbook, Elementary Spanish Chatbook and Business Spanish Chatbook along with audio CD's and Spanish Chatshow DVD's.
or order directly from our website:* SpanishChatCompany.com

INTRODUCCIÓN 4 CUATRO
QUERIDOS ESTUDIANTES = DEAR STUDENTS

EACH LESSON USES FOUR VERBS & THE FOLLOWING 10 CONVERSATIONAL ACTIVITIES:

1. **Empieza aquí** = Start here on pages 10, 20, 30, 40, 50 & 60
This is a chance to use the verbs correctly in controlled conversations by using the pronunciation guide in italics. This guide is meant to help a native English speaker read the Spanish phrase out loud. Each new word in the pronunciation guide is capitalized. For example, **mucho gusto** *(Moo-cho Goose-toh)* = nice to meet you. Two vowels combined into diphthongs are indicated by a slash: **Bien** = *(Bee/ehn)* = well/fine. A word with an accent mark means that the syllable is stressed and should be emphasized when spoken. For example, **teléfono** *(Teh-LEH-foh-noh)* = telephone the emphasis is on the second syllable "*LEH*"

2. **Con sus compañeros** = With your colleagues on pages 11, 21, 31, 41, 51, 61
This is a conversational partner activity. This book is primarily written in the polite "**usted**" form, most commonly spoken among adult acquaintances and used for customer service. "**Usted**" is pronounced *Oos-tehd*—like the oo in the word "moon." Our other books, *Culinary Spanish Chatbook* and *Elementary Spanish Chatbook,* are written in the informal "**tú**" which is used among friends and family.

3. **Yo sé los verbos** = I know the verbs on pages 12, 22, 32, 42, 52 & 62
This verb table highlights the verbs for the lesson. In the back of the book 60 verbs are listed in present tense, preterite and imperfect past tense for four different personal subjects. By learning the patterns of conjugation for these 12 common verbs, you will be able to apply these rules to conjugate any of your own verbs.

4. **Juegos** = Games on pages 13, 23, 33, 43, 53 & 63
An idea for practicing with your flashcards in a fun way.

5. **Gramática** = Grammar on pages 14, 24, 34, 44, 54 & 64
We will highlight one grammar topic in each lesson.

6. **Cultura** = Culture on pages 15, 25, 35, 45, 55 & 65
Trivia statements about each of the Spanish-speaking countries. Native speakers will have a variety of ways to say the same sentence. Just like we do in English when we say, "How are you?," "How are you doing?," "How is it going?" and "What's up?," none of the ways are wrong. They are just, different styles. Feel free to change and customize your conversations to fit the slang of your Hispanic acquaintances. We've tried to use correct Spanish without being too formal or too "Spanglish."

7. **Temas para conversar** = Conversational topics on pages 16, 26, 36, 46, 56 & 66
Create your own role play. You may use our suggested conversations or create your own.

8. **Tarea** = Homework on pages 17, 27, 37, 47, 57 & 67
This is a chance to increase your vocabulary.

9. **Más Tarea** = More homework on pages 18, 28, 38, 48, 58 & 68
Another activity to continue your learning.

10. **Ayúdame** = Help me on pages 19, 29, 39, 49, 59, & 69
A bonus chart or activity to extend your knowledge. The *Spanish Chatbook 2* aims to help you apply knowledge of Spanish immediately by personalizing the activities and making learning enjoyable. Have fun. You will make mistakes and you will survive. **¡Vámonos!** *(VAH-moh-nohs!)* = Let's go!

QUERIDOS MAESTROS = DEAR TEACHERS

INTRODUCCIÓN 5 CINCO

NECESITA = YOU WILL NEED:

- **Tijeras** = Scissors: one per student to cut out the flashcards

- **Sobre** = Envelope: one per student to keep the flashcards together

- **Dados** = Dice: one per every 2-3 students for some of the games

- **Instrumentos** = Instruments: one per student, if possible or one shaker to pass around the group

- **Pedazos** = Pieces: 16 small squares or dried beans for Bingo

- **Libros** = *Spanish Chatbook 2*: one per per student

- **Audio** = Audio CD: one per student, if possible, to enhance learning

- **Música Latina** = Latin Music: to play at the beginning of each lesson.

- **Recetas** = Recipes: You may want to have students sign up to bring a Hispanic appetizer and healthy snacks during each class. There are easy Latin American recipes in the back of this book on pages #70-72 = setenta hasta setenta y dos.

- **Paciencia** = Patience: Stay positive, stick to the lessons, tell students you will answer other questions before or after each session. Keep smiling!

LESSONS 1 & 4	LESSONS 2 & 5	LESSONS 3 & 6
PRESENT TENSE IN 1	**PRESENT TENSE IN 2**	**PRESENT TENSE IN 3**
PAST TENSE IN 4	**PAST TENSE IN 5**	**PAST TENSE IN 6**
HABLAR	COMER	ESTAR*
EMPEZAR*	VIVIR	SER*
TERMINAR	QUERER*	VER*
TRABAJAR	TENER*	IR*

*irregular verb

INTRODUCCIÓN 6 SEIS
FRASES POSITIVAS = POSITIVE PHRASES

PICK 3 OF THESE THAT DESCRIBE YOU. USE A NEW PHRASE EACH DAY!

YO ESTOY = I AM
USTED ESTÁ = YOU ARE (CHANGING)

- **bien** = well
- **lista(o)** = ready
- **muy bien** = very well
- **preparada(o)** = prepared

¡SE AMABLE! = BE KIND!
(MANY OF THESE COULD USE SER)

- **¡Bien hecho!** = Well done!
- **¡Brillante!** = Brilliant!
- **¡Buen trabajo!** = Good work!
- **¡Espectacular!** = Spectacular!
- **¡Excelente!** = Excellent!
- **¡Extraordinaria(o)!** = Extraordinary!
- **¡Fabuloso!** = Fabulous!
- **¡Fantástico!** = Fantastic!
- **¡Fenomenal!** = Phenomenal!
- **¡Impresionante!** = Impressive!
- **¡Increíble!** = Incredible!
- **¡Magnífico!** = Magnificent!
- **¡Maravilloso!** = Marvelous!
- **¡Muy bien!** = Very well!
- **¡Qué bien!** = Great!
- **¡Qué chévere!** = How cool! (South America)
- **¡Qué estupendo!** = Wonderful!
- **¡Qué guay!** = How cool! (Spain)
- **¡Qué padre!** = How cool! (Mexico)
- **¡Perfecto!** = Perfect!
- **¡Sobresaliente!** = Outstanding! (distinction)
- **¡Super!** = Super!

YO SOY = I AM
USTED ES = YOU ARE (PERMANENT)

- **admirable** = admirable
- **amable** = friendly
- **asombroso** = amazing
- **bonita(o)** = cute, pretty
- **buena(o)** = good
- **cortés** = courteous
- **especial** = special
- **excepcional** = exceptional
- **éxitosa(o)** = successful
- **fascinante** = fascinating
- **genial** = clever, great
- **ideal** = ideal, great
- **inteligente** = intelligent
- **lista(o)** = smart
- **orgullosa(o)** = proud
- **preciosa(o)** = precious, beautiful
- **puntual** = punctual
- **respetuosa(o)** = respectful
- **responsable** = responsible
- **sensacional** = sensational
- **simpática(o)** = nice
- **superior** = superior, top
- **un(a) ganador(a)** = winner
- **un(a) superestrella** = a superstar
- **único** = only, unique
- **valiente** = courageous

AUDIO CD TRACK LISTING

INTRODUCCIÓN 7 SIETE

Need a native speaker to pronounce the phrases?
Wish you could practice in the car or while exercising?
Would you like to reinforce what you've learned?
Want to hear these Spanish words pronounced correctly?

Our *Spanish Chatbook 2* CD/Audio tracks are now available. Enjoy listening to over 100 conversational phrases designed specifically to improve communication. Purchase the *Spanish Chatbook 2* CD/Audio tracks now to improve your pronunciation. Each time you see the Audio symbol in the book, you will be able to follow along to improve your Spanish skills. Native speakers will say the English question, then the English answer followed by the Spanish question and then allow you time to say the Spanish answer. Finally the speaker will give a possible Spanish answer and allow you time to repeat it. Listen to these questions, answers and conversations while driving, working, or exercising. Pair the book and audio together to maximize your learning experience! Order the CD/Audio tracks from our web site, SpanishChatCompany.com.

SPANISH CHATBOOK 2 AUDIO TRACKS

1. **Introduction to *Spanish Chatbook 2* CD/Audio**
2. Lesson 1 *p. 10* **Empieza = Start with -ar present tense verbs**
3. Lesson 1 *p. 11* **Compañeros = Collegues with -ar present tense verbs**
4. Lesson 1 *p. 16* **A conversation with -ar present tense verbs**
5. Lesson 2 *p. 20* **Empieza = Start with -er/-ir present tense verbs**
6. Lesson 2 *p. 21* **Compañeros = Collegues with -er/-ir present tense verbs**
7. Lesson 2 *p. 26* **A conversation with -er/-ir present tense verbs**
8. Lesson 3 *p. 30* **Empieza = Start with rulebreaker present tense verbs**
9. Lesson 3 *p. 31* **Compañeros = Collegues with rulebreaker present tense verbs**
10. Lesson 3 *p. 36* **A conversation with rulebreaker present tense verbs**
11. Lesson 4 *p. 40* **Empieza = Start with -ar imperfect and preterite past tense verbs**
12. Lesson 4 *p. 41* **Compañeros = Collegues with -ar imperfect and preterite past tense verbs**
13. Lesson 4 *p. 46* **A conversation with -ar imperfect and preterite past tense verbs**
14. Lesson 5 *p. 50* **Empieza = Start with -er/-ir imperfect and preterite past tense verbs**
15. Lesson 5 *p. 51* **Compañeros = Collegues with -er/-ir imperfect and preterite past tense verbs**
16. Lesson 5 *p. 56* **A conversation with -er/-ir imperfect and preterite past tense verbs**
17. Lesson 6 *p. 60* **Empieza = Start with rulebreaker past tense verbs**
18. Lesson 6 *p. 61* **Compañeros = Collegues with rulebreaker past tense verbs**
19. **Thank you and Final credits**

INTRODUCCIÓN 8 OCHO — NOMBRES = NAMES

Use the "Name" list to choose a Spanish name and write it on the line below. Some English names do not translate into Spanish, so you can use your middle name or choose a name that starts with the same letter as your name. Add your Spanish and English names to the name tag on the next page and decorate it using lots of bright colors. In Latin America, you would use two last names—your mother's maiden name and your father's name.

Me llamo _____. = My name is...
(Meh Yah-moh...)

MUJERES / DAMAS = WOMEN / LADIES

Adriana	Carolina	Gabriela	Lupe	Paula
Alejandra	Carlota	Gloria	Margarita	Rebeca
Alicia	Cecilia	Graciela	María	Raquel
Alma	Clara	Hilda	Maribel	Rosa
Amalia	Cristina	Inés	Maricarmen	Sandra
Ana	Diana	Isabel	Maricela	Sara
Andrea	Dora	Juana	Marisol	Sofía
Ángela	Elena	Julia	Marta	Susana
Beatriz	Esmeralda	Laura	Mercedes	Teresa
Blanca	Ester	Liliana	Mónica	Victoria
Carmen	Eva	Linda	Olga	Yolanda

HOMBRES / CABALLEROS = MEN / GENTLEMEN

Adán	Daniel	Gerardo	Juan	Pedro
Alberto	David	Gonzalo	Julio	Rafael
Alejandro	Diego	Gregorio	Luis	Ramón
Alfonso	Eduardo	Guillermo	Manuel	Raúl
Alfredo	Emilio	Héctor	Marcos	Roberto
Andrés	Enrique	Jaime	Mario	Rubén
Antonio	Ernesto	Javier	Mateo	Samuel
Arturo	Felipe	Jesús	Miguel	Santiago
Bernardo	Félix	Joaquín	Nicolás	Timoteo
Carlos	Fernando	Jorge	Oscar	Tomás
César	Francisco	José	Pablo	Victor

Recorta = Cut out along the dashed lines

LEARN SPANISH TODAY FOR WORK & PLAY

En español me llamo _____

(Spanish name)

My English name is _____

MAPA = MAP

INTRODUCCIÓN

9 NUEVE

This map highlights the 21 Spanish-speaking countries. Starting on the left of the front cover, here are the names corresponding to the flags of each country: Argentina, Bolivia, Chile, Nicaragua, Panama, Paraguay, Colombia, Uruguay, Venezuela, Mexico, Guatemala, Peru, Spain, El Salvador, Dominican Republic, Costa Rica, Cuba, Ecuador, Puerto Rico, Honduras, Equatorial Guinea.

Read the number chart across the rows to find patterns. Play a game called, "More or Less = Más o Menos." When having a tough day, Hispanics will answer the question, "¿Cómo está? = How are you?" with the reply, "más o menos." For our "más o menos" game you will need partners. One partner will think of a number between 1 and 1,000. The other person will then try to guess the number in Spanish. If the guessed number is too low, the partner will say, "más." If the guessed number is too high, the partner will say, "menos." Of course, all numbers guessed must be done in Spanish. For example, 492 = cuatrocientos noventa y dos.

LOS NÚMEROS = THE NUMBERS

COUNTING BY 1'S	COUNTING BY 1'S	COUNTING BY 10'S	COUNTING BY 100'S	COUNTING BY 1,000'S
1 uno (Oo-noh)	11 once (Ohn-seh)	10 diez (Dee/ehs)	100 cien (See/ehn) 110 ciento diez (See/ehn-toh Dee-ehs)	1000 mil (Meel)
2 dos (Dohs)	12 doce (Doh-seh)	20 veinte (Veh/een-teh)	200 doscientos (Doh-see/ehn-tohs)	2018 dos mil dieciocho (Dee/eh-see/oh-cho)
3 tres (Trehs)	13 trece (Treh-seh)	30 treinta (Treh/een-tah)	300 trescientos (Treh-see/ehn-tohs)	3.000 tres mil (Trehs Meel)
4 cuatro (Coo/ah-troh)	14 catorce (Kah-tohr-seh)	40 cuarenta (Coo/ah-rent-tah)	400 cuatrocientos (Coo/ah-troh-see/ehn-tohs)	4.000 cuatro mil (Coo/ah-troh Meel)
5 cinco (Seen-koh)	15 quince (Keen-seh)	50 cincuenta (Seen-qwehn-tah)	500 quinientos (Kee-nee/ehn-tohs)	5.000 cinco mil (Seen-koh Meel)
6 seis (Seh/ace)	16 dieciséis (Dee/eh-see-SEH/ace)	60 sesenta (Seh-sehn-tah)	600 seiscientos (Seh/ace-see/ehn-tohs)	6.000 seis mil (Seh/ace Meel)
7 siete (See/eh-teh)	17 diecisiete (Dee/eh-see-see/eh-teh)	70 setenta (Seh-tent-tah)	700 setecientos (Seh-teh-see/ehn-tohs)	7.000 siete mil (See/eh-teh Meel)
8 ocho (Oh-cho)	18 dieciocho (Dee/eh-see/oh-cho)	80 ochenta (Oh-chen-tah)	800 ochocientos (Oh-cho-see/ehn-tohs)	8.000 ocho mil (Oh-cho Meel)
9 nueve (Noo/eh-veh) 10 diez (Dee/ehs)	19 diecinueve (Dee/eh-see-noo/eh-veh)	90 noventa (Noh-vehnt-tah)	900 novecientos (Noh-veh-see/ehn-tohs)	9.000 nueve mil (Noo/eh-veh Meel)

LECCIÓN 1 LESSON

¿LISTOS PARA CHARLAR? =
Ready to chat?

Los Verbos en la Lección 1 son:

hablar = to talk / to speak

trabajar = to work

terminar = to finish / to end

empezar = to begin / to start

LECCIÓN 1
10 DIEZ

Begin by reviewing the vowels and then use these two conversation starters with the present tense **-ar** verbs. Student #1 asks the first question and Student #2 answers. Now Student #2 asks the first question and Student #3 answers. Continue until everyone has asked and answered the first question. Then move on to the next question. Use the glossary at the end of the book to help you change the underlined phrases to fit your own information

EMPIEZA AQUÍ = START HERE

VOCALES = VOWELS	PRONUNCIACIÓN = PRONUNCIATION	PALABRAS = WORDS
A	ah	**Hola.** = Hello.
E	eh	**¿Cómo se llama usted?** = What is your name?
I	eee	**Me llamo Julia. ¿Y usted?** = My name is Julie. And you?
O	oh	**Mucho gusto.** = Nice to meet you.
U	oo	**Hasta luego.** = See you later.

1. HABLAR = TO TALK-TO SPEAK
TENSE: PRESENT-AR VERB

"**¿Habla usted español?**"
(¿Ah-blah Oos-tehd Eh-spah-ñyohl?)
Do you speak Spanish?

"**Yo hablo <u>un poco</u> de español.**"
(Yoh Ah-bloh <u>Oon Poh-koh</u> Deh Eh-spah-ñyohl.)
I speak <u>a little</u> Spanish.

2. TRABAJAR = TO WORK
TENSE: PRESENT-AR VERB

"**¿Dónde trabaja usted?**"
(¿DOHN-deh Trah-bah-hah Oo-stehd?)
Where do you work?

"**Yo trabajo <u>en la compañía Spanish Chat.</u>**"
(Yoh Trah-bah-hoh <u>Ehn Lah Coh-pah-NEE/ah Spanish Chat.</u>)
I work <u>at Spanish Chat Company.</u>

TRACK 2

SPANISH CHATBOOK 2 © SPANISH CHAT COMPANY

LECCIÓN 1
11 ONCE

This activity will be completed with partners. These three sentences use present tense **-ar** verbs. You and your partner will do these final three conversation starters. Remember: **Poco a poco.** = Little by little, like baby steps.

CON SUS COMPAÑEROS = WITH YOUR COLLEAGUES

3. TRABAJAR = TO WORK
TENSE: PRESENT -AR VERB

"¿En qué trabaja usted?"
(¿Ehn KEH Trah-bah-hah Oo-stehd?)
In what do you work? (What job do you do?)

"Yo trabajo como <u>asistente</u>."
(Yoh Trah-bah-hoh Koh-moh Ah-sees-tehn-teh.)
I work as an assistant.

REPASO DEL TIEMPO = REVIEW OF TIME

a la una = at 1:00	siete y cuarto = 7:15	siete y media = 7:30	ocho menos cuarto = 7:45
a las dos, tres... = at 2:00, 3:00...	de la mañana = in the morning	de la tarde = in the afternoon/evening	de la noche = in the night

4. EMPEZAR = TO BEGIN-TO START
TENSE: PRESENT -AR VERB **STEM CHANGER -E-TO-IE**

"¿A qué hora empieza usted su día?"
(¿Ah KEH Oh-rah Ehm-pee/eh-zah Oo-stehd Soo Dee-ah?)
At what time do you begin your day?

"Yo empiezo mi día a las <u>ocho de la mañana</u>."
(Yoh Ehm-pee/eh-zoh Mee DEE/ah Ah Lahs <u>Oh-cho Deh Lah Mah-ñyah-nah</u>.)
I begin my day at <u>eight in the morning</u>.

5. TERMINAR = TO END-TO FINISH
TENSE: PRESENT -AR VERB

"¿A qué hora termina usted su día?"
(¿Ah KEH Oh-rah Tehr-mee-nah Oo-stehd Soo DEE-ah?)
At what time do you finish your day?

"Yo termino mi día a las <u>cinco de la tarde</u>."
(Yoh Tehr-mee-noh Mee DEE/ah Ah Lahs <u>Seen-koh Deh Lah Tahr-deh</u>.)
<u>I finish my day at five in the evening.</u>

© SPANISH CHAT COMPANY   SPANISH CHATBOOK 2

LECCIÓN 1
12 DOCE

How do these present tense verbs work? Cross off the **-ar** ending and underline the remainder, which is called the verb stem. Now add the correct ending to the stem. Watch out for the last verb **"empezar"** because the stem changes from **-e-** to **-ie-**. Memorize the ending patterns and practice with any other **-ar** verbs. Write a question and answer for each verb. The Answer Key has ideas to help you write your 4 questions and 4 answers. After you write them, practice with a partner.

YO SÉ LOS VERBOS = I KNOW THE VERBS

To conjugate in the present tense; first take off **-ar** to get the stem, then add:

yo = I Take off **-ar** = stem + **o**	**More than one subject:**
One subject:	**ustedes / ellos** =
ella / él / usted =	you plural / they Take off **-ar** = stem + **an**
she / he / you Take off **-ar** = stem + **a**	

IDEAS PARA LAS FRASES = IDEAS FOR SENTENCES

HABLAR = to talk / to speak	Yo hablo... = I speak	Ustedes hablan... = you all speak
	Usted habla... = You speak	
	¿Habla usted...? = (Do) you speak...?	¿Hablan ustedes...? = (Do) you all speak?

TRABAJAR = to work	Yo trabajo... = I work	Ellas trabajan... = they all (females) work
	Ella trabaja... = She works	
	¿Trabaja ella...? = (Does) she work?	¿Trabajan ellas...? = (Do) they all (females) work?

EMPEZAR* = to start / to begin *the stem changes from -e- to -ie-	Yo empiezo... = I begin	Ellos empiezan... = they all begin
	Él empieza... = He begins	
	¿Empieza él...? = (Does) he begin?	¿Empiezan ellos...? = (Do) they all begin?

TERMINAR = to finish / to end	Yo termino... = I finish	Juanito y Elena Rosa terminan... = (Jaden) John and Elena Rose finish
	Julia termina... = Julie finishes	
	¿Termina Francisco...? = (Does Brad) Francis finish?	¿Terminan Eliana, Natalia y Clara...? = (Do) Eliana, Natalie and Clara finish?

SPANISH CHATBOOK ❷

Cut these flashcards apart and play the **Tres en Raya** = Three in a Row /Tic Tac Toe game using the board on the following page, **página 13 = trece**. Strive to find at least five minutes each day to review the phrases on the flashcards. Bring them to class each week in an envelope or small bag. **La practica hace al maestro.** = Practice makes perfect.

Cut out the X & O pieces on the back of this page!

Recorta = Cut out along the dashed lines

YO HABLO UN POCO DE ESPAÑOL. = LECCIÓN 1	**¿HABLA USTED OTRO IDIOMA?** = LECCIÓN 1	**ELLOS SÓLO HABLAN INGLÉS.** = LECCIÓN 1
YO TRABAJO DURO COMO GERENTE DE UNA OFICINA. = LECCIÓN 1	**¿TRABAJA USTED MUCHO?** = LECCIÓN 1	**USTEDES TRABAJAN DEMASIADO.** = LECCIÓN 1
YO EMPIEZO MI TRABAJO A LAS SIETE DE LA MAÑANA. = LECCIÓN 1	**¿A QUÉ HORA EMPIEZA USTED SU TRABAJO?** = LECCIÓN 1	**MIS AMIGOS EMPIEZAN MUY TEMPRANO.** LECCIÓN 1
YO TERMINO A LAS SEIS DE LA TARDE. = LECCIÓN 1	**¿A QUÉ HORA TERMINA USTED?** = LECCIÓN 1	**MIS COMPAÑEROS TERMINAN SU TAREA PARA LA CLASE.** LECCIÓN 1

© SPANISH CHAT COMPANY

SPANISH CHATBOOK ❷

They only speak English. =	Do you speak another language? =	I speak a little Spanish.=
PRESENT TENSE	PRESENT TENSE	PRESENT TENSE
They work too much. =	Do you work a lot?=	I work hard as a manager of an office.=
PRESENT TENSE	PRESENT TENSE	PRESENT TENSE
My friends begin very early.=	At what time do you start your job? =	I start my work at seven in the morning. =
PRESENT TENSE	PRESENT TENSE	PRESENT TENSE
My acquaintances finish their homework for the class. =	At what time do you finish? =	I finish at six in the evening. =
PRESENT TENSE	PRESENT TENSE	PRESENT TENSE

SPANISH CHATBOOK ❷ © SPANISH CHAT COMPANY

To play **Tres en Raya** = Three-in-a-Row," you and your partner will share one board. Lay out nine flashcards with the Spanish side up. Try the English side for a challenge. Player X will go first by reading the Spanish sentence, then trying to say the English translation without looking at the back. If successful, Player X will cover and covering that square with an X piece. Next is Player O's turn. Take turns. Play until someone gets three in a row like "Tic-Tac-Toe."

LECCIÓN 1

13 | TRECE

JUEGO DE "TRES EN RAYA" = GAME OF "THREE-IN-A-ROW"

LECCIÓN 1
14 CATORCE

In the Spanish language each noun is either masculine or feminine. There are four ways to say "the:" **"el, la, los, las."** Complete these sentences using definite and indefinite articles, and then invent your own sentences using the correct articles.

GRAMÁTICA = GRAMMAR

Nombres y Artículos = Nouns & Articles

- Masculine nouns frequently end in –o –os –l –ma
- Feminine nouns frequently end with –a –as –dad –tad –tud –ción –sión
- Nouns ending in –ista and –e, can use either el, la, los, or las depending on gender. (La dentista & El dentista)
- Definite articles are the four ways of saying "the" = **la / el** are singular, **las / los** are plural
- Indefinite articles are the four ways of saying "a (an)" = **una / un** are singular, **unas / unos** are plural

ARTICLES	SINGULAR	PLURAL
FEMININE (DEFINITE)	**la** = the	**las** = the
FEMININE (INDEFINITE)	**una** = a / an	**unas / algunas** = some
MASCULINE (DEFINITE)	**el** = the	**los** = the
MASCULINE (INDEFINITE)	**un** = a / an	**unos / algunos** = some

1. _____ **niña termina la tarea.** = <u>The</u> girl finishes the homework.

2. _____ **niña termina su tarea.** = <u>A</u> girl finishes her homework.

3. _____ **niño no habla Inglés.** = <u>The</u> boy does not speak English.

4. _____ **niño no habla con extranjeros.** = <u>A</u> boy does not speak with foreigners.

5. _____ **estudiantes empiezan a trabajar.** = <u>The</u> all female students begin to work.

6. _____ **estudiantes empiezan a trabajar.** = <u>Some</u> all female students begin to work.

7. _____ **primos y tíos trabajan en** _____ **hoteles.** = <u>The</u> cousins and aunts/uncles work at <u>the</u> hotels.

8. _____ **primos y tíos trabajan en** _____ **hoteles.** = <u>Some</u> cousins and aunts/uncles work at <u>some</u> hotels.

LECCIÓN 1

15 QUINCE

Guess which two sentences are **cierto** = true and which one is **falso** = false for the **Lugares para visitar** = Places to visit, and then do the same for the **Días festivos** = Holidays. Take a group vote by holding up either one, two or three fingers to show which one you believe is false. Use the Answer Key to find out why.

CULTURA = CULTURE

ESPAÑA = SPAIN

Lugares para visitar en España = Places to visit in Spain

(C | F) **1.** En el museo El Prado en Madrid, los guías hablan sobre los artistas Goya, Picasso y Velázquez. =
In the Prado museum in Madrid, the guides talk about the artists Goya, Picasso and Velázquez.

(C | F) **2.** En Córdoba, la historia de un edificio importante empieza como una Mezquita y termina como una Catedral Católica. =
In Cordoba, the history of an important building begins as a Mosque and ends as a Catholic cathedral.

(C | F) **3.** Don Quijote y Sancho Panza trabajan en San Sebastián, España. =
Don Quijote and Sancho Panza work in San Sebastian, España.

Días festivos en España = Holidays in Spain

(C | F) **1.** Durante la Semana Santa en Sevilla, más de 50 personas trabajan juntas en el desfile para llevar a cuestas un "paso" hecho de madera. =
During the Holy week in Seville, more than 50 people work together in the parade to carry (on their backs) a "religious float" made (sculpted) from wood.

(C | F) **2.** El último miércoles de agosto, los turistas empiezan a tirar uvas en la calle para celebrar "La Tomatina" en Valencia. =
The last Wednesday of August, the tourists begin to throw grapes in the street to celebrate "The Tomatina" to celebrate in Valencia.

(C | F) **3.** En Pamplona, la fiesta del 7 al 14 de julio se llama "San Fermín." Los toros y la gente terminan de correr en la plaza de toros. –
In Pamplona, the holiday from July 7-14 is called "St. Fermin." The bulls and the people finish running at the bullring.

LECCIÓN 1
16 DIECISÉIS

Read the role play below and then invent your own. Imagine a similar situation when you need to communicate in Spanish. Maybe you are meeting a Spanish-speaker or helping someone complete a form. Use the questions and answers to help you create your scenario. Change the endings to fit for male or female characters. Practice a few times and then act out your conversation for the group as time allows.

TEMAS PARA CONVERSAR = CONVERSATIONAL TOPICS

TEMA: Tardanza = Tardiness
DICHO: Más vale tarde que nunca. = Better late than never.

SPANISH		ENGLISH	
LA AMIGA NUEVA (MUJER)	EL AMIGO NUEVO (HOMBRE)	THE NEW FRIEND (FEMALE)	THE NEW FRIEND (MALE)
Buenos Días. ¿Cómo se llama?	Me llamo José. ¿Y usted?	Good morning. What is your name?	My name is Joe. And you?
Me llamo Julia. Mucho gusto.	Mucho gusto. ¿Cuál es su apellido?	My name is Julie. Nice to meet you.	Nice to meet you. What is your last name?
Mi apellido es Pospishil.	¿Habla inglés?	My last name is Pospishil.	Do you speak English?
Hablo español y un poco de inglés.	¿Dónde trabaja usted?	I speak Spanish and a little English.	Where do you work?
Trabajo en un banco.	¿En qué trabaja usted?	I work in an bank.	What is your job?
Trabajo como gerente.	¿A que hora empieza su trabajo?	I work as a manager.	At what time does your job start?
Mi trabajo empieza a las 9 de la mañana.	¿A que hora termina su trabajo?	My job starts at 9 a.m.	At what time does your job finish?
Mi trabajo termina a las 4 de la tarde.	¿Entiende todo?	My job finishes at 4 p.m.	Do you understand everything?
No, no entiendo algunas preguntas.	Espere un momento, por favor, mientras busco un intérprete.	No, I don't understand some (of the) questions.	Wait one moment, please while I look for an interpreter.
Claro que sí. Hasta pronto.	Que tenga un buen día.	Yes of course. See you soon.	Have a great day.

SPANISH CHATBOOK 2 © SPANISH CHAT COMPANY

LECCIÓN 1

17 DIECISIETE

Your homework is to finish the next two pages and any exercises from Lesson 1. You may want to work ahead on Lesson 2 to be ready for the next class. Keep an eye out for any current events in the news this week about Spain. Translate the first six phrases into English and the last six phrases into Spanish.

TAREA = HOMEWORK

1. ¿Termina su hija con la comida? _____

2. Ellos hablan un poco de Inglés. _____

3. Yo trabajo cada día. _____

4. Él termina la tarjeta de invitación para la fiesta. _____

5. ¿A qué hora empieza su escuela? _____

6. Yo hablo por teléfono en mi oficina. _____

7. They finish their work. _____

8. Do you speak Spanish? _____

9. Where do you all work? _____

10. I begin to work at the house. _____

11. My son works at the museum. _____

12. When (do) they begin? _____

LECCIÓN 1
18 DIECIOCHO

This can be done as homework. Complete the crucigrama = crossword puzzle by using the correct verb conjugations. The Spanish verb will fit in the boxes exactly if it is correct. Check your answers in the Answer Key when you are finished.
¡Buena suerte! = Good luck!

UN POCO MÁS DE TAREA = A LITTLE MORE HOMEWORK

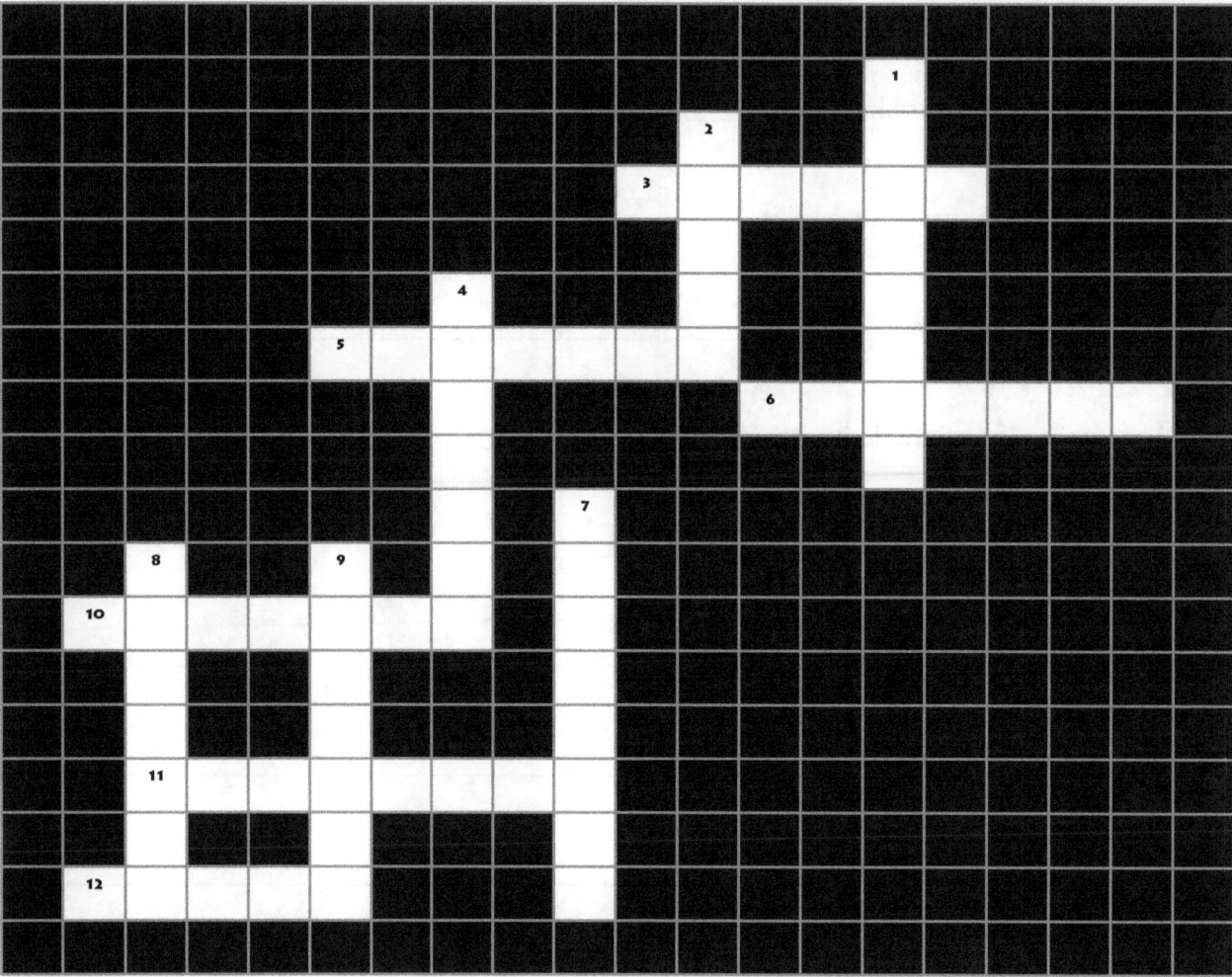

HORIZONTAL

3 they talk = **ellos** _____

5 I finish = **yo** _____

6 he works = **él** _____

10 I begin = **yo** _____

11 you all begin = **ustedes** _____

12 she talks = **ella** _____

VERTICAL

1 they work = **ellos** _____

2 I speak = **yo** _____

4 I work = **yo** _____

7 you all finish = **ustedes** _____

8 you begin = **usted** _____

9 you finish = **usted** _____

SPANISH CHATBOOK 2 © SPANISH CHAT COMPANY

Here is a bonus game to help you practice conjugating verbs. You can use it to review at the beginning or end of any lesson. Cut out the **rectangúlos** = rectangles below. Line up into two teams and give each team one set of game pieces. When the teacher says, "I work," the first person in each line races to hold up the correct cards, ie; **"trabaj"** and **"-o"**. You can also play individually with each person holding up their own cards.

LECCIÓN 1

19 DIECINUEVE

AYÚDAME POR FAVOR = HELP ME PLEASE

HABL-
(take off the **-ar** to get the stem)
LECCIÓN 1

-O
"**yo**" form of **-ar/-er-ir** verbs

-E
"**él** = he, **ella** = she, **usted** = you & one subject" form of **-er/-ir** verbs

---

TRABAJ-
(take off the **-ar** to get the stem)
LECCIÓN 1

-A
"**él** = he, **ella** = she, **usted** = you & one subject" form of **-ar** verbs

-EN
"**ellos** = they, **ustedes** = you all & more than one subject" form of **-er/-ir** verbs

---

EMPIEZ-
(take off the **-ar** to get the stem, then change the **-e** to **-ie**)
LECCIÓN 1

-AN
"**ellos** = they, **ustedes** = you all & more than one subject" form of **-ar** verbs

ADD YOUR OWN VERB STEMS USING THE CHARTS IN THE BACK OF THE BOOK

TERMIN-
(take off the **-ar** to get the stem)
LECCIÓN 1

QUIER-
(take off the **-er** to get the stem, then change the **-e** to **-ie**)
LECCIÓN 2

¡YO LO TENGO!
= I HAVE IT!

FOR A CHALLENGE TRY ADDING THE "NOSOTROS" AND "TU" VERB FORMS

VIV-
(take off the **-ir** to get the stem)
LECCIÓN 2

COM-
(take off the **-er** to get the stem)
LECCIÓN 2

TIEN-
(take off the **-er** to get the stem, then change the **-e** to **-ie**) Note: the "**yo**" form is "**tengo**."
LECCIÓN 2

© SPANISH CHAT COMPANY

SPANISH CHATBOOK ❷

LECCIÓN 2 LESSON

ES LA HORA DE CHARLAR. =
It is time to chat.

Los Verbos en la Lección 2 son:

vivir = to live

comer = to eat

querer = to want

tener = to have

LECCIÓN 2
20 VEINTE

Begin by reviewing the homework from Lesson 1. Now use these **-er/-ir** verbs as conversation starters for the entire group. Student #1 asks the first question and Student #2 answers. Now Student #2 asks the first question and Student #3 answers. Continue until everyone has asked and answered the first question. Then move on to the next question. Use the glossary at the end of the book to help you change the underlined phrases to fit your own information.

EMPIEZA AQUÍ = START HERE

1. VIVIR = TO LIVE

TENSE: PRESENT -IR VERB

"¿Dónde vive usted?"
(¿DOHN-deh Vee-veh Oo-stehd?)
Where do you live?

"Yo vivo en <u>la Ciudad de México</u>."
(Yoh Vee-voh Ehn <u>Lah See/oo-dahd Deh MEH-he-koh</u>.)
I live in <u>Mexico City</u>

2. QUERER = TO WANT

TENSE: PRESENT -ER VERB **STEM CHANGER -E-TO-IE**

"¿A dónde quiere viajar usted?"
(¿Ah DOHN-deh Kee/eh-reh Vee-ah-har Oo-stehd?)
To where do you want to travel?

"Yo quiero viajar a <u>España</u>."
(Yoh Kee/eh-roh Vee-ah-har Ah <u>Ehs-pah-ñyah</u>.)
I want to travel to <u>Spain.</u>

UN JUEGO = A GAME

Use the map on page 9 to play a game similiar to "battleship" called "Turistas" = "Tourists," draw a tiny turista near the name of one Spanish-speaking country that you would like to visit. Do not show your partner. For example, #1 draws a person by the word Ecuador and #2 draws a person by the word Cuba.
   #1 may say, "¿Quiere viajar a Venezuela?"
   Then #2 may say, "No, no quiero viajar a Venezuela. ¿Quiere viajar a Ecuador?"
Finally #1 says, Sí, yo quiero viajar a Ecuador. #1 and #2 are both trying to be the first one to find the tourist.

3. COMER = TO EAT

TENSE: PRESENT-ER VERB

"¿Come usted muchas frutas y verduras?"
(¿Koh-meh Oos-tehd Moo-chahs Froo-tahs Ee Vehr-doo-rahs?)
Do you eat lots of fruit and vegetables?

"Yo como muchas <u>fresas y manzanas</u>."
(Yoh Coh-moh Moo-chahs <u>Freh-sahs Ee Mahn-zah-nahs</u>.)
I eat lots of strawberries and apples.

TRACK 5

SPANISH CHATBOOK 2 © SPANISH CHAT COMPANY

This activity will be completed with partners. These three sentences use present tense -er verbs. You and your partner will do these final three conversation starters. Report back to the group by sharing one sentence in Spanish that you learned about a family member of your partner. **Bien hecho.** = Well done.

LECCIÓN 2
21 VEINTIUNO

CON SUS COMPAÑEROS = WITH YOUR COLLEAGUES

LA FAMILIA = THE FAMILY

una hermana menor = one younger sister	dos hermanas menores = two younger sisters	una hermana mayor = one older sister	cuatro hermanas mayores = four older sisters
un hermano menor = one younger brother	tres hermanos menores = three younger brothers (also could be three younger siblings)	un hermano mayor = one older brother	cinco hermanos mayores = five older brothers (also could be five older siblings)

4. TENER = TO HAVE

TENSE: PRESENT -ER VERB **STEM CHANGER -E-TO-IE**
EXCEPT YO CHANGES TO TENGO

"¿Tiene usted <u>hermanos menores</u>?"
(¿Tee/eh-neh Oo-stehd Ehr-mah-nohs Meh-nohr-ehs?)
Do you have younger siblings?

"Yo tengo <u>un hermano menor</u>."
(Yoh Tehn-goh <u>Oon Ehr-mah-noh Meh-nohr</u>.)
I have <u>one younger brother</u>.

5. TENER = TO HAVE

TENSE: PRESENT -ER VERB **STEM CHANGER -E-TO-IE**
EXCEPT YO CHANGES TO TENGO

"¿Tiene usted <u>hermanos mayores</u>?"
(¿Tee/eh-neh Oo-stehd Ehr-mah-nohs My-yohr-ehs?)
Do you have older siblings?

"Yo tengo dos hermanas mayores."
(Yoh Tehn-goh <u>Dohs Ehr-mah-nahs My-yohr-ehs</u>.)
I have <u>two older sisters</u>.

6. ¿MÁS FAMILIA? = MORE FAMILY?

NOW ASK ABOUT OTHER FAMILY MEMBERS

sobrina / sobrino = niece / nephew
prima / primo = female cousin / male cousin
nieta / nieto = granddaughter / grandson
nuera / yerno = daughter-in-law / son-in-law

hija / hijo = daughter / son
mascotas / perro / gato = pets / dog / cat
cuñada / cuñado = sister-in-law / brother-in-law
suegra / suegro = mother-in-law / father-in-law

© SPANISH CHAT COMPANY

LECCIÓN 2

22 VEINTIDÓS

How do these present tense verbs work? Cross off the **-er** or **-ir** ending and underline the remainder, which is called the verb stem. Now add the correct ending to the stem. Watch out for the stem changes in querer and tener. Memorize the ending patterns and practice with any other **-er/-ir** verbs. Also the verb **"tener"** changes to -go in the **"yo"** form making it a **-go -go** verb like those on page 29 = veintinueve. Write a question and answer for each verb and practice them with a partner. The Answer Key has ideas to help you write your questions.

YO SÉ LOS VERBOS = I KNOW THE VERBS

To conjugate in the present tense; first take off **-er/-ir** to get the stem, then add:

yo = I Take off **-er/-ir** = stem + **o**	**More than one subject:**
One subject:	**ustedes / ellos** =
ella / él / usted =	you plural / they Take off **-er/-ir** = stem + **en**
she / he / you Take off **-er/-ir** = stem + **e**	

IDEAS PARA LAS FRASES = IDEAS FOR SENTENCES

VIVIR = to live	**Yo vivo...** = I live	**Ustedes viven** = you all live
	Usted vive... = You live	**¿Viven ustedes...?** = (Do) you all live...?
	¿Vive usted...? = (Do) you live...?	
COMER = to eat	**Yo como...** = I eat	**Ellas comen...** = they all (females) eat
	Ella come... = She eats	**¿Comen ellas...?** = (Do) they all (females) eat...?
	¿Come ella...? = (Does) she eat...?	
QUERER* = to want / to wish *the stem changes from -e- to -ie-	**Yo quiero...** = I want	**Ellos quieren...** = they all want
	Él quiere... = He wants	**¿Quieren ellos...?** = (Do) they all want...?
	¿Quiere él...? = (Does) he want...?	
TENER* = to have *the stem changes from -e- to -ie- and the "yo" form is "tengo"	**Yo tengo...** = I have	**María Elena y Franco tienen...** = Mary Ellen and Frank have
	Mateo tiene... = Matt has	**¿Tienen Cintia, Tomás y Miguel...?** = (Do) Cindy, Tom and Michael have...?
	¿Tiene Diego...? = (Does) Doug have...?	

SPANISH CHATBOOK 2   © SPANISH CHAT COMPANY

Cut these flashcards apart to play the "**Toma Todo**" game described on the next page **23 = veinte y tres**. Get out a flashcard each day from your wallet to learn when you have a free minute or while you are waiting somewhere. Just like exercise, the more you work on it the better. Feel free to change the sentences to fit your lifestyle. For example, "Yo tengo 3 gatos."

Recorta = Cut out along the dashed lines

YO VIVO EN UNA CASA GRANDE. = LECCIÓN 2	**¿DÓNDE VIVE USTED?** = LECCIÓN 2	**ELLOS VIVEN EN UN APARTAMENTO PEQUEÑO.** = LECCIÓN 2
YO COMO MÁS FRUTAS QUE VERDURAS. = LECCIÓN 2	**¿COME USTED SUFICIENTES VERDURAS?** = LECCIÓN 2	**¿COMEN USTEDES DULCES CADA DÍA?** = LECCIÓN 2
YO QUIERO VIAJAR A AMÉRICA DEL SUR. = LECCIÓN 2	**¿A DÓNDE QUIERE VIAJAR USTED?** = LECCIÓN 2	**ELLOS QUIEREN TENER MUCHO DINERO.** LECCIÓN 2
YO TENGO DOS PERROS, UN PEZ Y UN GATO. = LECCIÓN 2	**¿TIENE USTED MASCOTAS?** = LECCIÓN 2	**MIS AMIGAS TIENEN HAMBRE Y SED.** LECCIÓN 2

They live in a small apartment. = *PRESENT TENSE*	Where do you live? = *PRESENT TENSE*	I live in a big house. = *PRESENT TENSE*
Do you all eat sweets(candies) every day?= *PRESENT TENSE*	Do you eat enough vegetables? = *PRESENT TENSE*	I eat more fruits than vegetables. = *PRESENT TENSE*
They want lots of money. = *PRESENT TENSE*	Where do you want to travel? *PRESENT TENSE*	I want to travel to South America. = *PRESENT TENSE*
My friends (all female) have thirst and hunger. (My friends are thirsty and hungry.)= *PRESENT TENSE*	Do you have pets? = *PRESENT TENSE*	I have two dogs, a fish and a cat. = *PRESENT TENSE*

SPANISH CHATBOOK ❷ © SPANISH CHAT COMPANY

Play the game **"Toma Todo** = Take Everything." Each player chooses six flashcards. When one person asks the question in Spanish, the other player answers in Spanish. The first person to run out of flashcards loses the game. This game can be played in partners, a group of three or by dividing the group into two teams.

LECCIÓN 2

23 VEINTITRÉS

UN JUEGO DE "TOMA TODO" = A GAME OF "TAKE EVERYTHING"

IF YOU ROLL A 1- TOMA 1 = TAKE 1
You take one from the center and say it in Spanish.

IF YOU ROLL A 2- TOMA 2 = TAKE 2
You take two from the center and say them in Spanish.

IF YOU ROLL A 3- PON 1 = PUT 1
You put one in the center and say it in Spanish.

IF YOU ROLL A 4- PON 2 = PUT 2
You put two in the center and say them in Spanish.

IF YOU ROLL A 5- TODOS PONEN = EVERYONE PUTS ONE
EACH player has to put one in the center and say it in Spanish

IF YOU ROLL A 6-*TOMA TODO* = TAKE EVERYTHING
¡Jackpot! Take all the pieces from the center and as an extra bonus you don't have to say anything.

© SPANISH CHAT COMPANY

SPANISH CHATBOOK ❷

LECCIÓN 2
24 VEINTICUATRO

There are positive and negative ways to reply in Spanish conversation. Complete these sentences using the affirmative and negative, then invent your own using these words. Note the double negative is translated into English using a parenthesis in order to honor our English teachers.

GRAMÁTICA = GRAMMAR

Positivo y Negativo = Positive and Negative

- In Spanish use double or triple negatives, **No, no queremos nada.** = No we (do not) want nothing.

- **Alguna/alguno** and **ninguna/ninguno** depend on the feminine or masculine noun that follows. **Algunas ciudades no tienen ninguna estación del autobus en el mapa.** = Some cities do have not one bus station on the map.

POSITIVO = POSITIVE	**NEGATIVO** = NEGATIVE
algo = something	**nada** = nothing
alguien = someone (in general)	**nadie** = no one (in general)
algún = some	**ningún** = no / none
alguna/alguno = some, somebody (refers to a specific noun)	**ninguna/ninguno** = none, nobody, not one (refers to a specific noun)
o...o = either...or	**ni...ni** = neither...nor
siempre = always	**nunca** = never
también = also (me too)	**tampoco** = also do not (me neither)

1. Sí, yo tengo _____ importante. = Yes, I have <u>something</u> important.

2. No, yo no tengo _____ importante. = No, I do (not) have <u>nothing</u> important.

3. Quiero limpiar mi escritorio casi _____. = I want to clean my desk almost <u>always</u>.

4. Quiero limpiar mi escritorio casi _____. = I want to clean my desk almost <u>never</u>.

5. Vivo con _____ en mi apartamento. = I live with <u>someone</u> in my apartment.

6. No vivo con _____ en mi apartamento. = I (don't) live with <u>no one</u> in my apartment.

7. No como en restaurantes caros y _____ tomo agua sin gas. = I don't eat at expensive restaurants and I <u>also do not</u> drink water without bubbles.

8. Yo _____ como en restaurantes caros y _____ tomo agua con gas. = I <u>neither</u> eat at expensive restaurants <u>nor</u> drink water with bubbles.

Guess which two sentences are **cierto** = true and which one is **falso** = false for the **Lugares para visitar** = Places to visit, and then do the same for the **Días festivos** = Holidays. Take a group vote by holding up either one, two or three fingers to show which one you believe is false. Use the Answer Key to find out why.

LECCIÓN 2
25 VEINTICINCO

CULTURA = CULTURE

MÉXICO = MEXICO

Lugares para visitar en México = Places to visit in Mexico

C | F **1.** En Teotihuacán, nadie vive en la Avenida de las Almas Vivas, entre las pirámides de la Luna y el Sol. =
In Teotihuacan, no one lives on the Avenue of the Living Souls, between the pyramids of the Moon and the Sun.

C | F **2.** Mucha gente quiere visitar al Templo Mayor, la Catedral y el Palacio Nacional en la plaza "Zócalo" en la Ciudad de México D.F. (Distrito Federal). =
Many people want to visit the Main Temple, the Cathedral and the National Palace in the Zocalo plaza in Mexico City (Federal District).

C | F **3.** En la Capital, usted tiene que ver la "Danza de los Voladores" y la "Piedra del Sol" en el Museo Nacional de Antropología. =
In the Capital, you have to see the "Dance of the Pole Flyers" and the "Sun Stone / Aztec Calendar" in the National Museum of Anthropology.

Días festivos en México = Holidays in Mexico

C | F **1.** Miguel Hidalgo es famoso por su grito "Viva México" en el Día de la Independencia, el 16 de septiembre. Él tiene el título de "Padre" en tres sentidos: Padre (sacerdote), Padre del País y padre de cinco hijos biológicos. =
Miguel Hidalgo is famous for his shout of "Long Live Mexico" on Independence Day, September 16. He has the title of "Father" in three ways: Father (priest), Father of the country and Father of five biological children.

C | F **2.** El 1 y 2 de noviembre, Día de los Muertos, las familias quieren comer Pan de Muerto y poner flores anaranjadas en el cementerio y en altares que se llaman "ofrendas." =
On November 1-2, Day of the Dead, families want to eat "Bread of the Dead" and put orange flowers at the cemetery and on altars that are called "offerings."

C | F **3.** Durante Las Posadas, los 12 días antes de la Navidad, ellos comen con sus vecinos y hacen piñatas para sus fiestas. =
During "The Lodging" the 12 days before Christmas, they eat with their neighbors and make piñatas for their parties.

LECCIÓN 2
26 VEINTISÉIS

Read the role play below aloud or invent your own. Imagine a similar situation when you could have inquired about a native Spanish speaker's family or assisted them with a project at work. Use the questions and answers to help you create your scenario. Practice a few times and then act out your conversation for the group as time allows.

TEMAS PARA CONVERSAR = CONVERSATIONAL TOPICS

TEMA: Las metas individuales vs. el grupo = Individual vs. Group goals
DICHO: Dígame con quién anda, y le diré quién es. = Tell me who you walk around with and I will tell you who you are. Also, birds of a feather flock together.

SPANISH		ENGLISH	
LAS PREGUNTAS	LAS RESPUESTAS	THE QUESTIONS	THE ANSWERS
¿En qué le puedo ayudar?	¿Puede ayudarme con el proyecto sobre mi familia?	How may I help you?	Can you help me with the project about my family?
Claro que sí. ¿Dónde vive usted?	Vivo en Omaha, Nebraska.	Yes of course. Where do you live?	I live in Omaha, NE.
¿Cuántos hermanos tiene?	Tengo seis hermanos.	How many siblings do you have?	I have six siblings.
¿Tiene hijos?	Sí. Tengo dos hijos.	Do you have children?	Yes. I have two children.
¿Cuántos años tienen sus hijos?	Mis hijos tienen 12 y 14 años.	How old are your children?	My children are 12 and 14 years old.
¿Tiene animales?	Tengo un pez, un perro, un caballo y dos gatos.	Do you have animals?	I have a fish, a dog, a horse and two cats.
¿Quiere hacer algo con su familia?	Quiero viajar a América Central con mi familia.	Do you want to do anything with your family?	I want to travel to Central America with my family.
¿Qué come usted para su cena favorita?	Yo como quesadillas con carne para mi cena favorita.	What do you eat for your favorite dinner?	I eat cheesy tortillas with meat for my favorite dinner.
¿Tiene fotos de su familia?	Sí. Tengo algunas aquí.	Do you have photos of your family?	Yes. I have some here.
Buen trabajo.	Gracias, hasta luego.	Good work.	Thank you, see you later.

TRACK 7

SPANISH CHATBOOK 2 © SPANISH CHAT COMPANY

LECCIÓN 2

27 VEINTISIETE

Your homework is to finish the next two pages and any exercises from Lesson 2. You may want to work ahead on Lesson 3 to be ready for the next group. Keep an eye out for any current events in the news this week about Mexico. Translate the first six phrases into English and the last six phrases into Spanish.

TAREA = HOMEWORK

1. Ustedes viven en los Estados Unidos de América. _____

2. ¿Nadie quiere comer sus verduras? _____

3. ¿Tienen ustedes algunas clases en la universidad? _____

4. Él nunca come arroz con pollo para su almuerzo. _____

5. Yo tengo mucha tarea. _____

6. ¿Vive usted cerca de alguna amiga? _____

7. My dogs always eat a lot. _____

8. I also do not live with my grandparents. _____

9. I want to work tomorrow also. _____

10. ¿You all want to eat something? _____

11. The family has dessert at 9 p.m. _____

12. I never eat nothing for breakfast. *(Spanish double negative)* _____

LECCIÓN 2

28 VEINTIOCHO

¿Qué es esto? = What is this? Now you have an opportunity to practice. Conjugate each verb in Spanish and write it on the line provided. Next find these Spanish verbs in the word search.

UN POCO MÁS DE TAREA = A LITTLE MORE HOMEWORK

```
É N O G N E T V R O M D N E I
C T Q U E I O T E N E M O S A
L O I H M V P A N E N E I T P
Á V M E M E D D I Á V E S G Á
E P V E N O M O C E N S Í O N
R M T M V E D U D T M T R L B
E Y A O I O N E Í E D E U P N
I L G V S N S C D O I M E S A
U D A I E E S A S U D A L R R
Q Z H V S Á R H Q Y Z B A O N
Ó D I E B R A D J S D M H S E
M V E Í E N E R A M V I V E M
I N E R E I U Q D I T O D E O
L P M N R C O M E L E N A O C
J U L I A V X A N J U L P U V
```

BUSCAPALABRAS = WORD SEARCH

1. he lives = **él** _____
2. I have = **yo** _____
3. they want = **ellos** _____
4. you all eat = **ustedes** _____
5. she wants = **ella** _____
6. I live = **yo** _____
7. you have = **usted** _____
8. I eat = **yo** _____
9. I want = **yo** _____
10. he eats = **él** _____
11. they have = **ellos** _____
12. you all live = **ustedes** _____

SPANISH CHATBOOK 2 © SPANISH CHAT COMPANY

On Page 22 = veintidós we learned that the verb **"tener"** changes to -go in the **"yo"** form. Spanish teachers call these **-go -go** verbs. Below is a list of some of the irregular present tense verbs called "-go-go" verbs. To remember these you can sing them to the melody of "The Farmer in the Dell."

LECCIÓN 2
29 VEINTINUEVE

AYÚDAME POR FAVOR = HELP ME PLEASE

-GO-GO VERBS	CANCIÓN = SONG
These verbs change to go in the -yo form	Sing this to the melody of "The Farmer in the Dell" to help you remember the go-go verbs.
decir = to say, tell (digo, dice, dicen) **caer** = to fall (caigo, cae, caen) **hacer** = to do, to make (hago, hace, hacen) **oír** = to hear (oigo, oye, oyen) **poner** = to put (pongo, pone, ponen) **salir** = to leave (salgo, sale, salen) **tener** = to have (tengo, tiene, tienen) **traer** = to bring/take/carry (traigo, trae, traen) **valer** = to value (valgo, vale, valen) **venir** = to come (vengo, viene, vienen)	digo, caigo, hago, oigo, pongo, salgo, tengo, traigo, valgo y vengo

LECCIÓN 3 LESSON

MÁS POR FAVOR.

More please.

Los Verbos en la Lección 3 son:

ir = to go

ver = to see

estar = to be (changing)

ser = to be (permanent)

LECCIÓN 3
30 TREINTA

Begin by reviewing the homework from Lesson 2. Review the differences between ser and estar using the chart below. Now use these **"rule breaker"** verbs as group conversation starters. Student #1 asks the first question and Student #2 answers. Now Student #2 asks the first question and Student #3 answers. Continue until everyone has asked and answered the first question. Then move on to the next question.

EMPIEZA AQUÍ = START HERE

ESTAR	SER
CHANGING	PERMANENT
Weather	Date
Emotion	Occupations
Change from Previous Condition	Time
Location	Characteristics That Are Permanent
Lifestyle	Origin / Nationality
Health	Mine / Posession

1. SER = TO BE (PERMANENT)
TENSE: PRESENT **RULE BREAKER**

"¿Cuándo es su cumpleaños?"
(¿Qwahn-doh Ehs Soo Koom-pleh-ah-ñyohs?)
When is your birthday?

"Mi cumpleaños es el 29 de noviembre."
(Mee Koom-pleh-ah-ñyohs Ehs Ehl Veh/ee-teh Ee Noo/eh-veh Deh Noh-vee/ehm-breh.)
My birthday is the 29th of November.

2. IR = TO GO
TENSE: PRESENT **RULE BREAKER**

"¿Va usted a algún lugar para descansar?"
(¿Vah Oo-stehd Ahl-GOON Loo-gahr Pah-rah Dehs-kahn-sahr?)
Do you go to some place to rest?

"Yo voy a la playa para descansar."
(Yoh Voh/ee Ah Lah Plah-yah Pah-rah Dehs-kahn-sahr.)
I go to the beach to rest.

TRACK 8

SPANISH CHATBOOK 2

This activity will be completed with partners during group. Ask and answer these three questions. If you and your partner finish, then continue onto the next activity.
Sigue intentando. = Keep trying..

LECCIÓN 3
31 TREINTA Y UNO

CON SUS COMPAÑEROS = WITH YOUR COLLEAGUES

3. VER = TO SEE
TENSE: PRESENT **RULE BREAKER**

"No veo el reloj. ¿Qué hora es?"
(Noh Veh/oh Ehl Reh-loh. KEH Oh-rah Ehs?)
I don't see the clock. What time is it?

"Yo veo que <u>son las tres de la tarde</u>."
(Yo veh/oh keh <u>Sohn Lahs Trehs Deh Lah Tahr-deh</u>.)
I see that it is <u>3:00 in the afternoon</u>. *(See Lesson 1 p.11 for a review of times.)*

4. ESTAR = TO BE (CHANGING)
TENSE: PRESENT **RULE BREAKER**

"¿Dónde está el baño?"
(¿DohN-deh Ehs-TAH Ehl Bah-ñyoh?)
Where is the bathroom?

"El baño está por <u>este pasillo a la derecha</u>."
(Ehl Bah-ñyoh Ehs-TAH Pohr <u>Ehs-teh Pah-see-yoh Ah Lah Deh-reh-chah</u>.)
The bathroom is down <u>this hall on the right</u>.

5. SER = TO BE (PERMANENT)
TENSE: PRESENT **RULE BREAKER**

"¿De dónde es usted?"
(¿De DohN-deh Ehs Oo-stehd?)
Where are you from (where were you born)?

"Yo soy de <u>los Estados Unidos de América</u>."
(Yoh Soy Deh <u>Lohs Eh-stah-dohs Oon-ee-dohs Deh Ah-MEH-ree-kah</u>.)
I am from <u>the United States of America</u>.

LECCIÓN 3

32 TREINTA Y DOS

How do these present tense verbs work? These verbs are very common but break all of the rules and do not follow the normal patterns like regular verbs. You will just have to memorize these. Write a question and answer for each verb and practice them with a partner. The Answer Key has ideas to help you write your questions. Watch out for the stem changers and the changers in the **"yo"** form.

YO SÉ LOS VERBOS = I KNOW THE VERBS

To conjugate in the present tense; first take off **-ar** to get the stem, then add:

yo = I Take off --ar/-er/-ir = stem + o	**More than one subject:**
One subject:	**ustedes / ellos** =
ella / él / usted =	you plural / they
she / he / you	
Take off **-ar** = stem + **a** OR Take off **-er/-ir** = stem + **e**	Take off **-ar** = stem + **an** Take off **-er/-ir** = stem + **en**

IDEAS PARA LAS FRASES = IDEAS FOR SENTENCES

IR* = to go *memorize this one	**Yo voy...** = I go	**Ustedes van...** = you all go
	Usted va... = You go	**¿Van ustedes...?** = (Do) you all go...?
	¿Va usted...? = (Do) you go...?	

VER* = to see *the stem is the letter V & The "yo" form is "veo"	**Yo veo...** = I see	**Ellas ven...** = they all (females) see
	Ella ve... = She sees	**¿Ven ellas...?** = (Do) they all (females) see...?
	¿Ve ella...? = (Does) she see...?	

ESTAR* = to be (changing) *the "yo" form is "estoy" Add accents to "está" & "están"-	**Yo estoy...** = I am	**Ellos son...** = they all are
	Él es... = He is	**¿Son ellos...?** = Are they...?
	¿Es él...? = Is he...?	

SER* = to be (permanent) **memorize this one	**Yo soy...** = I am	**Carolina y Melchor son...** = Carolyn and Merle are
	Catalina es... = (Sharre) Kate is	**¿Son Emilia y Mateo...?** = Are Emily and Matt...?
	¿Es Andrés...? = Is Andrew ...?	

Cut these flashcards apart and play "Around the World" described on **página 33 = treinta y tres**. Find someone to practice with and set aside 10 minutes a day to practice together or schedule a weekly "Spanish lunch." Bring in different Hispanic foods and speak Spanish.

Recorta = Cut out along the dashed lines

YO VEO QUE SON LAS SIETE DE LA MAÑANA. = LECCIÓN 2	**¿VE USTED UN RELOJ? ¿QUÉ HORA ES?** = LECCIÓN 2	**USTEDES SIEMPRE VEN LAS PELÍCULAS NUEVAS.** = LECCIÓN 2
YO VOY A LAS MONTAÑAS PARA VACACIONES. = LECCIÓN 2	**¿VA USTED A ALGÚN LUGAR?** = LECCIÓN 2	**ELLOS VAN A LA PLAYA A DESCANSAR.** = LECCIÓN 2
YO ESTOY MUY OCUPADA(O). = LECCIÓN 2	**¿DÓNDE ESTÁ EL BAÑO?** = LECCIÓN 2	**LOS BAÑOS ESTÁN POR ESTE PASILLO A LA IZQUIERDA.** = LECCIÓN 2
YO SOY DE LOS ESTADOS UNIDOS DE AMÉRICA. (EE.UU.) = LECCIÓN 2	**¿DE DÓNDE ES USTED?** = LECCIÓN 2	**MIS MESES FAVORITOS SON NOVIEMBRE Y DICIEMBRE.** = LECCIÓN 2

© SPANISH CHAT COMPANY

You all always see the new movies.= PRESENT TENSE	Do you see a clock? What time is it?= PRESENT TENSE	I see that it is 7:00 in the morning.= PRESENT TENSE
They go to the beach to rest. = PRESENT TENSE	Will you go to some place?= PRESENT TENSE	I go to the mountains for vacation.= PRESENT TENSE
The bathrooms are down this hall on the left. PRESENT TENSE	Where is the bathroom? = PRESENT TENSE	I am very busy. = PRESENT TENSE
My favorite months are November and December. PRESENT TENSE	Where are you from? (originally) = PRESENT TENSE	I am from the United States of America. (U.S.A.) = PRESENT TENSE

SPANISH CHATBOOK ❷ © SPANISH CHAT COMPANY

Select one of these eight final projects. Either present these during the final lesson and/or share them with Hispanic employees or Spanish-speaking friends. Then play **"Alrededor del Mundo** = Around the World" explained at the bottom of the page.

LECCIÓN 3
33 TREINTA Y TRES

PROYECTOS FINALES = FINAL PROJECTS

- **The theater = El teatro:** Roleplay a typical exchange with a Spanish speaker or a comical customer service experience. Do this alone or with a partner and use props or exaggerate to make this funny. Each person should say about 10 lines. Have a native speaker check your script before your presentation.

- **The important phrases = Las frases importantes:** Make your own list of 15 phrases you will use most. Type these in English and Spanish. (Add the pronunciation if it helps you.) Either take these from the phrases in the lessons or invent your own. Make a small "cheat sheet" to keep with you or make a poster to hang in your kitchen.

- **In the kitchen = En la cocina:** Write out at least 12 sentences in Spanish for a cooking show script. Include the ingredients and the steps to the recipe as you are preparing the food. Either videotape this cooking show to watch in two weeks or demonstrate it live. Find recipes on pages #70-72 = setenta hasta setenta y dos.

- **The map = El mapa:** Write out at least 12 sentences that give us a tour of your home or workplace. Use directional words such as **norte, sur, oeste, este, a la derecha and a la izquierda**. Design a map and print it from your computer, or use a video camera and give us a walking tour in Spanish.

- **The story = El cuento:** This could be a mini-book with at least 12 sentences about any topic of your choice. It could be about Hispanic holidays, a trip, or even a book about a typical day.

- **The travel agency = La agencia de viajes:** You are a travel agent advertising your country so people will want to come to visit. You could also plan an itinerary for a 3-5 day trip. Make a brochure, poster or computer presentation about your country.

- **Have any other ideas? = ¿Tiene alguna otra idea?:** Create any other meaningful project with at least 12-15 phrases in Spanish that will help you the most in your life.

ALREDEDOR DEL MUNDO = AROUND THE WORLD

Using any flashcards or the verb rectangles from page 19 = diecinueve, play the game called **"Alrededor del Mundo** = Around the World." The host/teacher will say the phrase in English. One student will stand behind the chair of another student. These two students will compete to be the first person to correctly say the phrase in Spanish. The rest of the group will listen and wait for their turn. The winner is the first of the two students that is able to shout out the phrase, even if they have to look it up in their book. The rest of the group is silent. The winner advances to the next student on the right, and those two compete to say the phrase in Spanish first. Play continues all the way "around the room/world." The person that defeats the most opponents is declared the winner.

LECCIÓN 3

34 TREINTA Y CUATRO

Complete these sentences using possessive adjectives and possessive pronouns, then invent your own. A quick grammar reminder: a possessive adjective shows ownership and describes a noun. A possessive pronoun takes the place of a noun and shows who owns something.

GRAMÁTICA = GRAMMAR

Posesivos = Possessive (Adjectives & Pronouns)

- Examples of possessive adjectives:
  A Santiago le gusta <u>mi</u> trabajo. = James likes <u>my</u> work.
  A ellos no les gusta <u>su</u> trabajo. = They do not like <u>their</u> work.

- Examples of possessive pronouns:
  A Rosa le gusta <u>el suyo.</u> = Rose likes <u>hers</u>.
  A ellos les gusta <u>los suyos</u>. = They like <u>theirs</u>.

ARTICLES	SINGULAR	PLURAL
POSSESSIVE ADJECTIVE	**mi** = my **su** = your, his, her, its, their **nuestra / nuestro** = our	**mis** = my **sus** = your, his, her, its, their **nuestras / nuestros** = our
FEMININE POSSESSIVE PRONOUN	**mía** = mine **suya** = yours, hers, theirs **nuestra** = ours	**mías** = mine **suyas** = yours, hers, theirs **nuestras** = ours
MASCULINE POSSESSIVE PRONOUN	**mío** = mine **suyo** = yours, his, theirs **nuestro** = ours	**míos** = mine **suyos** = yours, his, theirs **nuestros** = ours

1. Natalia es _____ sobrina. = Natalie is <u>my</u> niece.

2. Mi hermana dice, "Natalia es la_____." = My sister says, "Natalia is mine."

3. _____ sobrino Miguel está en un partido de fútbol. = <u>His</u> nephew Michael is in a soccer game.

4. Los equipos_____ ganan mucho. = The teams of <u>his</u> win a lot.

5. _____ hombres y mujeres trabajadores van al almuerzo. = <u>Our</u> men and women workers go to lunch.

6. Ellos ven las frutas y dicen "son las _____." = They see the fruits and say, "they're <u>ours</u>."

Guess which two sentences are **cierto** = true and which one is **falso** = false for the **Lugares para visitar** = Places to visit, and then do the same for the **Días festivos** = Holidays. Take a group vote by holding up either one, two or three fingers to show which one you believe is false. Use the Answer Key to find out why.

CULTURA = CULTURE

AMÉRICA CENTRAL = CENTRAL AMERICA
GUATEMALA | EL SALVADOR | HONDURUS | NICARAGUA | COSTA RICA | PANAMÁ

Lugares para visitar en América Central = Places to visit in Central America

(C | F) 1. En el bosque tropical lluvioso en Costa Rica con 100% de humedad, los expertos ven las más de 10,000 especies de plantas, árboles y animales. =
In the tropical rainforest in Costa Rica with 100% humidity, experts see more than 10,000 species of plants, trees and animals.

(C | F) 2. Ellos van a estar en un barco por más o menos dos horas para pasar por el canal de Panamá. =
They will be in a boat for more or less two hours to pass through the Panama Canal.

(C | F) 3. Tres volcanes están cerca de Antigua, Guatemala: Volcán de Agua, Volcán de Fuego y Acatenango con el pico que se llama "Las Tres Hermanas." =
Three volcanoes are close to Antigua, Guatemala: Water Volcano, Fire Volcano and Acatenango with the peak that is called "The Three Sisters."

Días festivos en América Central = Holidays in Central America

(C | F) 1. Todas las fiestas de Independencia de cualquier país de América Central son el 15 de septiembre. =
All the Independence Day celebrations of every Central American country are held on September 15.

(C | F) 2. El viernes antes de Pascua en Copán, Honduras, se ven muchas obras de arte maravillosas hechas en flores sobre las calles. =
The Friday before Easter in Copan, Honduras, you see many marvelous works of art made out of flowers (laying) on the streets.

(C | F) 3. En Nicaragua, la gente bailan con cintas alrededor del Palo de Mayo en el festival. Es muy divertido. =
In Nicaragua, people dance with ribbons around the Maypole in the festival. It is very fun.

LECCIÓN 3

36 TREINTA Y SEIS

Read the role play below or invent your own. Imagine a similar situation when you wanted to connect with Spanish-speakers that are coming to the front desk or you may have needed directions while traveling abroad. Use the questions and answers to help you create your scenario. Change the endings to fit for male or female characters. Act out your conversation for the group as time allows.

TEMAS PARA CONVERSAR = CONVERSATIONAL TOPICS

TEMA: Comportamientos y Recursos = Behaviors and Resources
DICHO: Entre dicho y hecho hay un buen trecho. =
Between word and deed there is a big gap.

SPANISH		ENGLISH	
EL CAJERO	LA CLIENTE	THE MALE CASHIER	THE FEMALE CLIENT
Bienvenida. Gracias por su paciencia.	De nada.	Welcome (to a female). Thank you for your patience.	You're welcome.
¿Cómo está usted?	Yo estoy más o menos bien.	How are you?	I am more or less O.K.
¿Cuándo es la cita?	La cita es el martes a las tres de la tarde.	When is the appointment?	The appointment is Tuesday at 3 p.m.
¿Cuál es su dirección?	Mi dirección es Calle 9 número 1117.	What is your address?	My address is Street 9 house number 1117.
¿Cuál es su número de teléfono?	Mi número de teléfono es (5-5-5) 4-10-13-19.	What is your phone number?	My phone number is (5-5-5) 4-10-13-19.
¿Cómo se dice "sign here" en español?	Se dice, "firme aquí."	How do you say "sign here" in Spanish?	You say, "sign here."
Entonces, firme aquí. ¿Necesita algo más?	Sí. Yo tengo una pregunta. ¿Dónde está el baño?	Then, sign here. Do you need anything else?	Yes. I have a question. Where is the bathroom?
El baño está allá. Buenas noches. Gracias por venir.	Que tenga un buen fin de semana. Adiós.	The bathroom is over there. Good night. Thank you for coming.	Have a great weekend. Goodbye.

SPANISH CHATBOOK 2 © SPANISH CHAT COMPANY

LECCIÓN 3

37 TREINTA Y SIETE

Your homework is to finish the next two pages and any exercises from Lesson 3. You may want to work ahead on Lesson 4.. Keep an eye out for any current events in the news this week about Central America. For the activity below, match the Spanish sentence with the corresponding English sentence. There are some new travel words.

UN POCO MÁS DE TAREA = A LITTLE MORE HOMEWORK

A (ah) For a porter it is not hard to lift a lot of luggage up the tall stairs.

B (beh) The girls are great dancers with their flags and their beautiful dresses of many colors.

C (seh) My poor boss is in bad health.

D (deh) I am going to change money at the next cashier.

E (eh) The 15 minute break is to drink a (small) coffee.

F (ehf-feh) They see nice wait staff who receive good tips.

G (heh) The passenger is on the airplane.

H (ah-cheh) The travel agents go to many parts of the world.

I (eee) The pedestrians are quite possibly in danger with so many cars downtown.

J (hoh-tah) He sees the map at the train station.

1. Mi pobre jefe está mal de salud.
2. La pasajera está en el avión.
3. Él ve el mapa en la estación del tren.
4. Los peatones están en posible peligro con tantos carros en el centro.
5. Para el portero no es difícil subir mucho equipaje por las escaleras altas.
6. Las chicas son buenas bailarinas con sus banderas y sus vestidos bonitos de muchos colores.
7. Voy a cambiar dinero en el próximo cajero.
8. Ellos ven meseros simpáticos que reciben buenas propinas.
9. Los 15 minutos de descanso son para tomar un cafecito.
10. Los agentes de viajes van a muchas partes del mundo.

LECCIÓN 3

38 TREINTA Y OCHO

Begin working on your final project. For the homework below, use the correct verb conjugations to fill in the squares, then use the letter from the black outlined square to make secret hidden words at the bottom of the page. You made it half way through the book. **Felicitaciones.** = Congratulations.

TAREA = HOMEWORK

1. I am tired. (changing) =
   Yo _____ cansada.

2. She goes to the office. =
   Ella _____ a la oficina.

3. I see another way. =
   Yo _____ otra manera.

4. They go fast. =
   Ellos _____ rápido.

5. Nice to meet you. =
   _____ gusto.

6. I am a teacher. =
   Yo _____ una maestra.

7. They are tall. =
   Ellos _____ altos.

    1 2   3 4 5 6 7

LECCIÓN 3

39 TREINTA Y NUEVE

Write your own three questions using this chart of all of the Present tense verbs found in this book. Share these by asking someone your three questions and answering their questions. Then switch partners as time allows. On the back of this page is an interview which you can use as an exam or simply to practice with native speakers at home or at your job.

AYÚDAME POR FAVOR = HELP ME PLEASE

INFINITIVE FORM TO...	I = YO FORM PRESENT TENSE (SPANISH)	ENGLISH	ONE SUBJECT = ELLA, ÉL, USTED FORM PRESENT TENSE (SPANISH)	ENGLISH	YOU PLURAL/THEY = USTEDES/ELLOS FORM PRESENT TENSE (SPANISH)	ENGLISH
EMPEZAR	yo empiezo	I begin / start	él empieza	he begins / starts	ellos empiezan	they begin
TERMINAR	yo termino	I finish / end	Julia termina	Julie finishes / ends	ustedes terminan	you all finish
HABLAR	yo hablo	I speak / talk	usted habla	you speak / talk	Carlota, Mateo y Emilia hablan	Sharre, Matt and Emily talk
TRABAJAR	yo trabajo	I work	Paco trabaja	Brad works	ellos trabajan	they work
COMER	yo como	I eat	usted come	you eat	ustedes comen	you all eat
QUERER	yo quiero	I want	ella quiere	she wants	ustedes quieren	you all want
TENER	yo tengo	I have	él tiene	he has	Cintia, Tomás y Miguel tienen	Cindy, Tom & Michael have
VIVIR	yo vivo	I live	usted vive	you live	ellos viven	they live
IR	yo voy	I go	él va	he goes	Melchor y Carolina van	Merle and Carolyn go
VER	yo veo	I see	usted ve	you see	Natalia y Eliana ven	Natalie and Eliana see
ESTAR	yo estoy	I am (changing)	Andres está	Andrew is (changing)	ellos están	they are
SER	yo soy	I am (permanent)	Diego es	Doug is (permanent)	ustedes son	you all are

© SPANISH CHAT COMPANY

SPANISH CHATBOOK 2

ENTREVISTA = INTERVIEW

SPANISH		ENGLISH	
PREGUNTA	RESPUESTA	QUESTION	ANSWER
Buenos Días. ¿Cómo se llama?	Me llamo Julia. ¿Y usted?	Good morning. What is your name?	My name is Julie. And you?
Me llamo José.	Mucho gusto.	My name is Joe.	Nice to meet you.
¿Cómo se escribe su apellido?	Mi apellido se escribe... P...O...S...	How do you write/spell your last name?	My last name is spelled/written...
¿Habla inglés?	Hablo mucho inglés.	Do you speak English?	I speak a lot of English.
¿Entiende español?	Entiendo un poco de español.	Do you understand Spanish?	I understand a little Spanish.
¿Dónde trabaja?	Trabajo como maestra de primer grado.	Where do you work?	I work as a First grade teacher. (Female)
¿Cómo está usted?	Estoy bien.	How are you?	I am fine.
¿Qué hora es?	Son las seis y media.	What time is it?	It is 6:30.
¿Le gusta la comida aquí?	Sí, me gusta. La comida es rica.	Do you like the food here.	Yes I like it. The food is tasty.
¿Cúal es su comida favorita?	Mi comida favorita es...	What is your favorite food?	My favorite food is...
¿Cúal es su bebida favorita?	Mi bebida favorita es...	What is your favorite drink?	My favorite drink is..
¿Cuántas personas hay en su familia?	Tengo cuatro personas en mi familia.	How many people are there in your family?	I have four people in my family.
¿Tiene animales?	Sí. Tengo un gato y un perro.	Do you have animals?	Yes. I have a cat and a dog.
¿Cuál es la fecha de hoy?	La fecha es el 16 de febrero.	What is the date today?	The date is the February 16.
¿Qué día es hoy?	Hoy es miércoles.	What day is today?	Today is Wednesday.
¿Cuándo es su cumpleaños?	Mi cumpleaños es el 15 de marzo.	When is your birthday?	My birthday is March 15.
¿Cuántos años tiene?	Tengo t'cinco años.	How old are you?	I am +5 years old.
¿Cómo está el clima hoy?	Hace sol y calor. O Hace viento y frío.	What is the weather like today?	It is sunny and hot. OR It is windy and cold.
¿Cuál es su número de teléfono?	Mi número de teléfono es (402)....	What is your phone number?	My phone number is..
¿Cuál es su dirección?	Mi dirección es...	What is your address?	My address is...
¿Dónde está el baño?	El baño está allí.	Where is the bathroom?	The bathroom is over there.
¿Cómo se dice "help me" en español?	Se dice, "ayúdame" o "socorro."	How do you say, "help me" in Spanish.	You say....

LECCIÓN 4 LESSON

SIGUE CHARLANDO. =

Keep chatting.

Los Verbos en la Lección 4 son:

hablar = to talk / to speak

trabajar = to work

terminar = to finish / to end

empezar = to begin / to start

LECCIÓN 4

40 CUARENTA

Begin by reviewing the homework from Lesson 3. Now use these Preterite PAST TENSE -**ar** verbs as conversation starters for the entire group. Student #1 asks the first question and Student #2 answers. Now Student #2 asks the first question and Student #3 answers. Continue until everyone has asked and answered the first question. Then move on to the next question. Look at the chart on page 49 = **cuarenta y nueve** for examples of words that signal if you should use preterite or imperfect.

EMPIEZA AQUÍ = START HERE

BEGIN CHATTING ABOUT THE PAST WITH TWO DIFFERENT TENSES

PRETERITE	IMPERFECT
English = done / did / -ed ending Look for words that indicate a specific time in the past	English = I used to / was / were -ing ending Descriptions of backgrounds, emotional state, ongoing events, habits and age

1. HABLAR = TO TALK-TO SPEAK
TENSE: PRETERITE PAST-AR VERB

"¿Habló usted español durante la semana pasada?"
(¿Ah-BLOH Oos-tehd Eh-spah-ñyohl Doo-rahn-teh Lah Seh-mah-nah Pah-sah-dah?)
Did you speak Spanish during the past week?

"Yo hablé <u>mucho (un poco de)</u> español <u>con mi jefe</u>."
(Yoh Ah-BLEH Moo-cho (Oon Poh-koh Deh) Eh-spah-ñyohl <u>Cohn Mee Heh-feh</u>.)
I spoke <u>a lot of (a little)</u> Spanish with <u>my boss</u>.

2. EMPEZAR = TO START- TO BEGIN
TENSE: PRETERITE PAST-AR VERB

"¿Cuándo empezó usted a trabajar por primera vez? ¿Y dónde?"
(¿Kwan-doh Ehm-peh-ZOH Ah Trah-bah-hahr Oo-stehd Pohr Pree-mehr-ah Vehs?¿ Ee DOHN-deh?)
When did you start work for the first time? And where?

"Yo empecé a trabajar en <u>un restaurante</u> como <u>mesera(o)</u>."
(Yoh Ehm-peh-SEH Ah Trah-bah-hahr Ehn <u>Oon Rehs-tah-rah-teh</u> Koh-moh <u>Meh-seh-rah</u>.)
I started to work at <u>a restaurant</u> as <u>a server</u>.

SPANISH CHATBOOK 2 © SPANISH CHAT COMPANY

This activity will be completed with partners. These three sentences use IMPERFECT PAST TENSE -ar verbs. You and your partner will do these final three conversation starters. **Maravilloso.** = Marvelous.

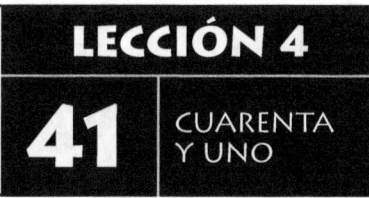

LECCIÓN 4
41 CUARENTA Y UNO

CON SUS COMPAÑEROS = WITH YOUR COLLEAGUES

3. HABLAR = TO TALK-TO SPEAK
TENSE: IMPERFECT PAST-AR VERB

"¿Qué idiomas hablaban sus parientes?"
(¿KEH Ee-dee/oh-mahs Ah-blah-bahn Soos Pah-ree/ehn-tehs?)
What languages did your relatives used to speak?

"Mis parientes hablaban inglés y alemán."
(Mees Pah-ree/ehn-tehs Ah-blah-bahn Een-GLEHS Ee Ah-leh-MAHN.)
My relatives spoke English and German.

4. TRABAJAR = TO WORK
TENSE: IMPERFECT PAST-AR VERB

"¿En qué clase de la universidad trabajaba duro usted cada día?"
(¿Ehn KEH Klah-seh Deh Lah Oo-nee-vehr-see-dad Trah-bah-hah-bah Doo-roh Oo-stehd Kah-dah DEE/ah?)
In what University class did you used to work hard every day?

"Yo trabajaba duro cada día en la clase de matemáticas."
(Yoh Trah-bah-ha-bah Doo-roh Kah-dah DEE/ah Ehn Lah Klah-seh Deh Mah-teh-MAH-tee-kahs.)
I worked hard every day in Math class.

5. TERMINAR = TO FINISH- TO END
TENSE: IMPERFECT PAST-AR VERB

"¿Cuáles proyectos no terminaba usted todavía?"
(¿Kwah-lehs Pro-yehk-tohs No Tehr-mee-nah-bah Oo-stehd Toh-dah-VEE-ah?)
Which of your projects did you still not finish?

"Yo todavía no terminaba mi álbum de fotos."
(Yoh Toh-dah-VEE-ah No Tehr-mee-nah-bah Mee AHL-boom Deh Foh-tohs.)
I still did not finish my photo album.

TO CONJUGATE IN THE PAST TENSE; FIRST TAKE OFF **-AR** TO GET THE STEM, THEN ADD:

SUBJECT	PRETERITE	IMPERFECT
yo = I	stem + **é**	stem + **aba**
ella / él / usted = she / he / you — *one subject*	stem + **ó**	stem + **aba**
ustedes / ellos = you plural / they — *more than one subject*	stem + **aron**	stem + **aban**

LECCIÓN 4
42 CUARENTA Y DOS

How do these past tense verbs work? Cross off the **-ar** ending and underline the remainder, which is called the verb stem. Now add the correct ending to the stem. Write a question and answer for each verb. Remember to put the verb first when writing a question. See the question examples from the charts on pages 12, 22 & 32. The Answer Key has ideas to help you write your 4 questions and 4 answers. Page 49 has clue words for Preterite vs. Imperfect. After you write them, practice with a partner.

YO SÉ LOS VERBOS = I KNOW THE VERBS

IDEAS PARA LAS FRASES = IDEAS FOR SENTENCES

HABLAR = spoke / used to speak	**P** Yo hablé	**P** Ustedes hablaron
	I Yo hablaba	**I** Ustedes hablaban
	P Usted habló	
	I Usted hablaba	

TERMINAR = finished / used to finish	**P** Yo terminé	**P** Ellas terminaron
	I Yo terminaba	**I** Ellas terminaban
	P Ella terminó	
	I Ella terminaba	

TRABAJAR = worked / used to work	**P** Yo trabajé	**P** Ellos trabajaron
	I Yo trabajaba	**I** Ellos trabajaban
	P Él trabajó	
	I Él trabajaba	

EMPEZAR* = began / used to begin **preterite z changes to c- in the yo form*	**P** Yo empecé	**P** Elena y Juan empezaron
	I Yo empezaba	**I** Ellen y John empezaban
	P Laura empezó	
	I Laura empezaba	

P = Preterite
I = Imperfect

SPANISH CHATBOOK 2

Cut these flashcards apart. The only thing that changes is the verb in each sentences because one side is preterite and the other side is imperfect. Remember that preterite is over and done with and imperfect continued or involved emotions. Put a date on your calendar to get your flashcards out and use them to review.

Recorta = Cut out along the dashed lines

YO TERMINÉ EL EXAMEN.
= I finished the exam.

PRETERITE LECCIÓN 4

¿TERMINÓ USTED? =
Did you finish?

PRETERITE LECCIÓN 4

USTEDES TERMINARON DE COMER. =
You all finished eat(-ing).

PRETERITE LECCIÓN 4

YO HABLÉ POR TELÉFONO. =
I spoke by telephone.

PRETERITE LECCIÓN 4

¿HABLÓ USTED CON ELLA? =
Did you speak with her?

PRETERITE LECCIÓN 4

ELLOS HABLARON ESPAÑOL. =
They spoke Spanish.

PRETERITE LECCIÓN 4

YO EMPECÉ A TRABAJAR.
= I started to work.

PRETERITE LECCIÓN 4

¿CUÁNDO EMPEZÓ USTED A TRABAJAR? =
When did you start to work?

PRETERITE LECCIÓN 4

ELLAS EMPEZARON A JUGAR FÚTBOL. =
They (all female) started to play soccer.

PRETERITE LECCIÓN 4

YO TRABAJÉ AQUÍ. =
I worked here.

PRETERITE LECCIÓN 4

¿TRABAJÓ USTED AQUÍ? =
Did you work here?

PRETERITE LECCIÓN 4

ELLOS TRABAJARON A LAS 11 DE LA MAÑANA.
= They worked at 11 a.m.

PRETERITE LECCIÓN 4

© SPANISH CHAT COMPANY

USTEDES TERMINABAN DE COMER. = You all finished eat(ing). *IMPERFECT LECCIÓN 4*	**¿TERMINABA USTED?** = Did you finish? *IMPERFECT LECCIÓN 4*	**YO TERMINABA EL EXAMEN.** = I finished the exam. *IMPERFECT LECCIÓN 4*
ELLOS HABLABAN... ESPAÑOL. = They spoke Spanish. *IMPERFECT LECCIÓN 4*	**¿HABLABA USTED CON ELLA?** = Did you speak with her? *IMPERFECT LECCIÓN 4*	**YO HABLABA POR TELÉFONO.** = I spoke by telephone. *IMPERFECT LECCIÓN 4*
ELLAS EMPEZABAN A JUGAR FÚTBOL. = They (all female) started to play soccer. *IMPERFECT LECCIÓN 4*	**¿CUÁNDO EMPEZABA USTED A TRABAJAR?** = When did you start to work? *IMPERFECT LECCIÓN 4*	**YO EMPEZABA A TRABAJAR.** = I started to work. *IMPERFECT LECCIÓN 4*
ELLOS TRABAJABAN A LAS 11 DE LA MAÑANA. = They worked at 11 a.m. *IMPERFECT LECCIÓN 4*	**¿TRABAJABA USTED AQUÍ?** = Did you work here? *IMPERFECT LECCIÓN 4*	**YO TRABAJABA AQUÍ.** = I worked here. *IMPERFECT LECCIÓN 4*

Play the "**Verbos y Dados** = Verbs and Dice" game. Select six flashcards and put them in the six rectangles below with either side facing up. Roll the dice. Change the verb in the sentence from Preterite to Imperfect or vice versa and then remove the flashcard. The first person to remove all six flashcards wins. You have to roll the number in the gray box to get to remove that particular flashcard.

LECCIÓN 4

43 CUARENTA Y TRES

EL JUEGO DE "VERBOS Y DADOS" =
THE GAME OF VERBS & DICE

TIRA UNA 1	TIRA UNA 2	TIRA UNA 3
TIRA UNA 4	TIRA UNA 5	TIRA UNA 6

LECCIÓN 4
44 CUARENTA Y CUATRO

Complete these sentences using demonstrative adjectives and pronouns. A quick grammar reminder: A demonstrative shows an object's location relative to the speaker. Note that demonstrative adjectives and pronouns have the same forms.

GRAMÁTICA = GRAMMAR

Demonstrativo = Demonstrative (Adjectives & Pronouns)

- Examples of demonstrative adjectives: **Esas** mujeres empezaron a hablar con la consejera ayer. = Those women began to talk with the counselor yesterday.

- Examples of demonstrative pronouns: Yo trabajaba a menudo en **este** proyecto. = I often worked on this project.

  Yo trabajaba a menudo en **este**. = I often worked on this one.

	SINGULAR	PLURAL
FEMININE DEMONSTRATIVE PRONOUNS & ADJECTIVES	**esta** = this one **esa** = that one **aquella** = that one over there	**estas** = these **esas** = those **aquellas** = those over there
MASCULINE DEMONSTRATIVE PRONOUNS & ADJECTIVES	**este** = this one **ese** = that one **aquel** = that one over there	**estos** = these **esos** = those **aquellos** = those over there

1. La asistente hablaba todo el tiempo sobre los problemas con _____ directora. =
The assistant talked all the time about the problems with that female principal (way over there).

2. En_____ momento _____ estudiantes hablaron en voces altas. =
At that moment those (male and female) students talked in loud voices.

3. Antes de ayer _____ enfermera trabajó. =
The day before yesterday this female nurse worked.

4. _____ escuelas primarias están llenas. =
Those (over there) elementary schools are full.

Guess which two sentences are **cierto** = true and which one is **falso** = false for the **Lugares para visitar** = Places to visit, and then do the same for the **Días festivos** = Holidays. Take a group vote by holding up either one, two or three fingers to show which one you believe is false. Use the Answer Key to find out why.

CULTURA = CULTURE

AMÉRICA DEL SUR = SOUTH AMERICA
BOLIVIA | COLOMBIA | ECUADOR | VENEZUELA | PERÚ

Lugares para visitar en América del Sur = Places to visit in South America

(C | F) 1. **En La Paz, Bolivia, la capital más alta del mundo, ellos terminaron de construir la carretera "más peligrosa del mundo."** =
In La Paz, Bolivia, the highest capital in the world, they finished building the "most dangerous highway in the world."

(C | F) 2. **El alcalde de Cartagena, Colombia, habló sobre sus famosos edificios modernos.** =
The mayor of Cartagena, Colombia, talked about their famous modern buildings.

(C | F) 3. **En la Mitad del Mundo, Ecuador, su GPS (sistema de posicionamiento global) siempre trabajaba perfectamente en el reloj del sol.** =
In "Middle of the World," Ecuador, your GPS always worked perfectly at the sundial.

Días festivos en América del Sur = Holidays in South America

(C | F) 1. **En Venezuela, el 24 de julio, los ciudadanos generalmente no trabajaban en el "Día del Natalicio del Libertador" en honor al hombre Che Guevara.** =
In Venezuela, on July 24, the citizens generally (have) not worked on the "Day of the Birth of the Liberator" in honor of Che Guevara.

(C | F) 2. **Hace muchos años en Colombia, terminaron la fiesta del "Año Viejo" con un muñeco hecho de ropa vieja con pólvora adentro. En Perú, cuando empezaron el Año Nuevo, unos comieron 12 uvas y corrieron afuera con sus maletas y otros se vistieron con ropa interior amarilla para la buena suerte.** = Many years ago in Colombia, they ended the party for the "Old Year" with a doll made of old clothes with firework powder inside. In Peru, when they began the New Year, some people ate 12 grapes and ran outside with their suitcases and others wore yellow underwear for good luck.

(C | F) 3. **El 24 de junio de cada año en Cuzco, Perú, mientras la gente miraba a los 500 actores en la fiesta de Inti Raymi, los guías hablaban sobre las costumbres de los Incas.** =
Every year on June 24 each year in Cuzco, Peru, while the people watched the 500 actors for the fiesta of Inti Raymi (Sun God), the guides talked about the customs of the Incas.

LECCIÓN 4
46 CUARENTA Y SEIS

Read the role play aloud or invent your own. Imagine a similar situation when a manager or a principal had to speak with Spanish-speakers about tardiness or absences. Use the questions and answers to help you create your scenario. Change the endings to fit for male or female characters. Practice a few times and then act out your conversation for the group.

TEMAS PARA CONVERSAR = CONVERSATIONAL TOPICS

TEMA: Ausencias = Absences
DICHO: Al mal tiempo, buena cara. =
In the bad times, put on a good face.

SPANISH		ENGLISH	
LA GERENTE	EL TRABAJADOR	THE FEMALE MANAGER	THE MALE WORKER
Buenas noches. ¿Quién es?	Habla José.	Good night. Who is it?	Joe speaks (speaking).
¿Con quién habló usted el mes pasado sobre sus ausencias?	Yo hablé con la directora.	Whom did you talk with last month about your absences?	I talked with the director (principal).
¿Trabajaba usted siempre en el día o en la noche?	Yo siempre trabajaba durante la noche.	Have you always worked in the day or in the night?	I have always worked during the night.
¿Por qué usted no trabajó ayer?	Yo no trabajé ayer porque mi carro no funcionó.	Why didn't you work yesterday?	I did not work yesterday because my car does not function.
¿A qué hora empezó su trabajo antes de ayer?	Empecé mi trabajo antes de ayer a las nueve de la noche.	At what time did you begin your work the day before yesterday?	I began work the day before yesterday at nine at night.
¿A qué hora terminó su trabajo antes de ayer?	Terminé antes de ayer a las cinco de la mañana.	At what time did you finish your work the day before yesterday?	I finished the day before yesterday at five in the morning.
Buena suerte. Que le vaya bien.	Gracias. A usted también.	Good luck. Hope all goes well.	Thank you. And you also.

SPANISH CHATBOOK 2 © SPANISH CHAT COMPANY

LECCIÓN 4

47 CUARENTA Y SIETE

Your homework is to finish the next two pages. Keep an eye out for any current events in the news this week about South America. For this activity you will be doing two things. First finish the sentence in Spanish and then write the English equivalent for the entire sentence.

TAREA = HOMEWORK

1. Hace un mes yo empecé a... _____

2. Yo empezaba .. _____

3. Él siempre empezaba...cuando... _____

4. Después que yo trabajé... _____

5. Ayer ustedes trabajaron en... _____

6. Ustedes trabajaban muchas veces... _____

7. Yo terminaba todos los días con... _____

8. Anoche ella terminó ... _____

9. Ella a veces terminaba sin... _____

10. Esta mañana usted habló (con/en/sobre/a)... _____

11. La otra semana ellos hablaron... _____

12. Cuando ellos hablaban entonces... _____

LECCIÓN 4
48 CUARENTA Y OCHO

This can be done as homework. Complete the crucigrama = crossword puzzle by using the correct verb conjugations. The Spanish verb will fit in the boxes exactly if it is correct. Check your answers in the Answer Key when you are finished. ¡Buena suerte! = Good luck!

HORIZONTAL (PRETERITE)

2 I began = **yo** _____

5 I spoke = **yo** _____

6 the children talked = **los niños** _____

8 you worked = **usted** _____

10 you all worked = **ustedes** _____

12 Elena & Jaden began = **Elena y Jaden** _____

VERTICAL (IMPERFECT)

1 they used to begin = **ellas** _____

3 I used to speak = **yo** _____

4 you all used to talk = **ustedes** _____

7 they used to work = **ellos** _____

9 you used to work = **usted** _____

11 I used to finish = **yo** _____

SPANISH CHATBOOK 2 © SPANISH CHAT COMPANY

Use this chart as a guide to help you find the words that signal when to use Preterite or Imperfect past tense. You may make a few mistakes, but keep trying and eventually the correct form will sound natural to you. Don't give up.

LECCIÓN 4

AYÚDAME POR FAVOR = HELP ME PLEASE

PRETERITE	IMPERFECT
English = done / did / -ed ending Look for these words that indicate a specific time in the past Think of a still photograph/snapshot of a past event	**English = I used to / was / were -ing ending** Descriptions of backgrounds, emotional state, ongoing events, habits and age Think of a home movie of a past event
a las ocho de la mañana = at 8 a.m.	**a menudo** = often
ayer = yesterday	**a veces** = sometimes
ayer por la tarde = yesterday afternoon	**cada día** = each / every day
antes de ayer = the day before yesterday	**cada semana** = each / every week
anoche = last night	**con frecuencia** = frequently
el año pasado = the past year	**cuando** = when
el mes pasado = the past month	**de vez en cuando** = from time to time
el otro día = the other day	**generalmente** = generally
entonces = then	**mientras** = while
en ese momento = at that moment	**muchas veces** = many times
el último mes = the last month	**mucho** = a lot
esta mañana = this morning	**siempre** = always
hace siete años = seven years ago	**todo el tiempo** = all the time
hace un mes = a month ago	**todos los días** = every day
la semana pasada = the past week	**usualmente** = usually

LECCIÓN 5 LESSON

CHARLAMOS UNA VEZ MÁS. =

Let's chat one more time.

Los Verbos en la Lección 5 son:

vivir = to live

comer = to eat

querer = to want

tener = to have

LECCIÓN 5
50 CINCUENTA

Begin by reviewing the homework from Lesson 4. Now use these Preterite PAST TENSE **-er/-ir** verbs as conversation starters for the entire group. Student #1 asks the first question and Student #2 answers. Now Student #2 asks the first question and Student #3 answers. Continue until everyone has asked and answered the first question. Then move on to the next question.

EMPIEZA AQUÍ = START HERE

1. TENER = TO HAVE
TENSE: PRETERITE PAST -ER/-IR VERB

"¿Cuándo tuvo usted prisa?"
(¿KWAHN-doh Too-voh Oo-stehd Pree-sah?)
When were you in a hurry?

"Yo tuve prisa cuando <u>me desperté tarde</u>."
(Yoh Too-veh Pree-sah Kwahn-doh <u>Meh Dehs-pehr-TEH Tahr-deh</u>.)
I was in a hurry when <u>I woke up late.</u>

2. COMER = TO EAT
TENSE: PRETERITE PAST-ER VERB

"¿Qué comió usted ayer?"
(¿KEH Koh-mee/OH Oo-stehd Ah-yehr?)
What did you eat yesterday?

"Ayer yo comí <u>arroz con pollo</u>."
(Ah-yehr Yoh Koh-MEE <u>Ahr-rrohs Kohn Poh-yoh</u>.)
Yesterday I ate <u>rice with chicken</u>.

COMIDA = FOOD

yogur con frutas = yogurt with fruit	**un sándwich con jamón** = a ham sandwich
ensalada con verduras = salad with vegetables	**un postre rico** = a tasty dessert
cereal con leche = cereal with milk	**papas fritas** = French fries
huevos revueltos = scrambled eggs	**hamburguesa con queso** = cheeseburger

SPANISH CHATBOOK 2

This activity will be completed with partners. These three sentences use IMPERFECT PAST TENSE **-er/-ir** verbs. You and your partner will do these final three conversation starters. **Sobresaliente.** = Outstanding.

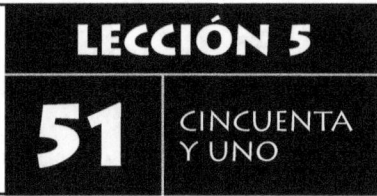

LECCIÓN 5

51 CINCUENTA Y UNO

CON SUS COMPAÑEROS = WITH YOUR COLLEAGUES

3. TENER / VIVIR = TO HAVE / TO LIVE   TENSE: IMPERFECT PAST -ER/-IR VERB

"¿Dónde vivía usted cuando tenía <u>siete</u> años?"
(¿DOHN-deh Vee-VEE/ah Oo/stehd Kwan-doh Teh-NEE/ah <u>See/eh-teh</u> Ah-ñyohs?)
Where did you live when you were <u>seven</u> years old? (had seven years)

"Yo vivía en <u>América del Sur</u> cuando tenía <u>siete</u> años."
(Yoh Vee-VEE/ah Ehn <u>Ah-MEH-ree-kah Dehl Soor</u> Kwan-doh Teh-NEE/ah <u>See/eh-teh</u> Ah-ñyohs.)
I lived in <u>South America</u> when I was <u>seven</u> years old.

4. COMER = TO EAT   TENSE: IMPERFECT PAST-ER VERB

"¿Qué comía usted a menudo los días festivos?"
(¿KEH Co-MEE/ah Oo-stehd Ah Meh-noo-doh Lohs DEE/ahs Fehs-tee-vohs?)
What did you often eat for (the) holidays?

"Para los días festivos yo comía <u>pavo con puré de papas</u>."
(Pah-rah Lohs DEE/ahs Fehs-tee-vohs Yoh Co-MEE/ah <u>Pah-voh Kohn Poo-REH Deh Pah-pahs</u>.)
For the holidays I often ate <u>turkey with mashed potatoes</u>.

5. QUERER = TO WANT / TO WISH   TENSE: IMPERFECT PAST-ER VERB

"¿Qué quería usted siempre?"
(¿KEH Keh-REE/ah Oo-stehd See/ehm-preh?)
What did you always want?

"Yo siempre quería <u>un millón de dólares</u>."
(Yoh See/ehm-preh Keh-REE/ah <u>Oon Mee-YOHN Deh DOH-lah-rehs</u>.)
I always wanted <u>a million dollars</u>.

TRACK 15

FOR PAST TENSE CONJUGATION; FIRST TAKE OFF **-ER/-IR** TO GET THE STEM, THEN ADD:

SUBJECT	PRETERITE	IMPERFECT
yo = I	stem + **í**	stem + **ía**
ella / él / usted = she / he / you — *one subject*	stem + **ió**	stem + **ía**
ustedes / ellos = you plural / they — *more than one subject*	stem + **ieron**	stem + **ían**

© SPANISH CHAT COMPANY   SPANISH CHATBOOK ❷

LECCIÓN 5

52 CINCUENTA Y DOS

How do these past tense verbs work? Cross off the **-er/-ir** ending and underline the remainder, which is called the verb stem. Now add the correct ending to the stem. Write a question and answer for each verb. Remember to put the verb first when writing a question. See the question examples from the charts on pages 12, 22 & 32. The Answer Key has ideas to help you write your 4 questions and 4 answers. Page 49 has clue words for Preterite vs. Imperfect. After you write them, practice with a partner.

YO SÉ LOS VERBOS = I KNOW THE VERBS

IDEAS PARA LAS FRASES = IDEAS FOR SENTENCES

COMER = ate / used to eat
- **P** Yo comí
- **I** Yo comía
- **P** Usted comió
- **I** Usted comía
- **P** Ustedes comieron
- **I** Ustedes comían

VIVIR = lived / used to live
- **P** Yo viví
- **I** Yo vivía
- **P** Ella vivió
- **I** Ella vivía
- **P** Ellas vivieron
- **I** Ellas vivían

QUERER* = wanted / used to want / wished for

*preterite -stem changes to -uis the yo form ends in e and there are no accents
- **P** Yo quise
- **I** Yo quería
- **P** Él quiso
- **I** Él quería
- **P** Ellos quisieron
- **I** Ellos querían

TENER* = had / used to have

*preterite stem changes to -uv - the yo form ends in e and there are no accents
- **P** Yo tuve
- **I** Yo tenía
- **P** Andrés tuvo
- **I** Andrew tenía
- **P** Carina y Miguelito tuvieron
- **I** Carrie y Mike tenían

P = Preterite
I = Imperfect

Cut these game pieces apart. Play "Las Parejas" = " The Pairs" a Matching/ Concentration game with the flashcards by matching the preterite with the imperfect as described on page 53 = **cincuenta y tres**. <u>Hint: The English sentences are the same so match the English together.</u>

Recorta = Cut out along the dashed lines

YO COMÍ ARROZ CON POLLO. = I ate chicken and rice. *PRETERITE LECCIÓN 5*	**¿QUÉ COMIÓ USTED?** = What did you eat? *PRETERITE LECCIÓN 5*	**USTEDES COMIERON JUNTOS.** = You all ate together. *PRETERITE LECCIÓN 5*
YO COMÍA ARROZ CON POLLO. = I ate chicken and rice. *IMPERFECT LECCIÓN 5*	**¿QUÉ COMÍA USTED?** = What did you eat? *IMPERFECT LECCIÓN 5*	**USTEDES COMÍAN JUNTOS.** = You all ate together. *IMPERFECT LECCIÓN 5*
YO VIVÍ CERCA DEL SUPERMERCADO. = I lived close to the supermarket. *PRETERITE LECCIÓN 5*	**¿DÓNDE VIVIÓ USTED?** = Where did you live? *PRETERITE LECCIÓN 5*	**ELLOS VIVIERON LEJOS.** = They lived far. *PRETERITE LECCIÓN 5*
YO VIVÍA CERCA DEL SUPERMERCADO. = I lived close to the supermarket. *IMPERFECT LECCIÓN 5*	**¿DÓNDE VIVÍA USTED?** = Where did you live? *IMPERFECT LECCIÓN 5*	**ELLOS VIVÍAN LEJOS.** = They lived far. *IMPERFECT LECCIÓN 5*
YO TUVE HAMBRE. = I had hunger. (was hungry) *PRETERITE LECCIÓN 5*	**¿TUVO USTED SED?** = Did you have thirst? (were you thirsty?) *PRETERITE LECCIÓN 5*	**ELLOS TUVIERON PRISA.** = They had hurry. (were in a hurry.) *PRETERITE LECCIÓN 5*
YO TENÍA HAMBRE. = I had hunger. (was hungry) *IMPERFECT LECCIÓN 5*	**¿TENÍA USTED SED?** = Did you have thirst? (were you thirsty?) *IMPERFECT LECCIÓN 5*	**ELLOS TENÍAN PRISA.** = They had hurry. (were in a hurry.) *IMPERFECT LECCIÓN 5*
YO QUISE TOMAR UNA SIESTA. = I wanted to take a nap. *PRETERITE LECCIÓN 5*	**¿QUISO USTED IR DE VACACIONES?** = Did you want to go on vacation? *PRETERITE LECCIÓN 5*	**ELLOS QUISIERON TENER UNA FIESTA.** = They wanted to have a party. *PRETERITE LECCIÓN 5*
YO QUERÍA TOMAR UNA SIESTA. = I wanted to take a nap. *IMPERFECT LECCIÓN 5*	**¿QUERÍA USTED IR DE VACACIONES?** = Did you want to go on vacation? *IMPERFECT LECCIÓN 5*	**ELLOS QUERÍAN TENER UNA FIESTA.** = They wanted to have a party. *IMPERFECT LECCIÓN 5*

© SPANISH CHAT COMPANY

SPANISH CHATBOOK ❷

SPANISH CHATBOOK 2

Pick any 12 game pieces from the previous page (6 pairs) and place them on the game board below. Play "**Las Parejas** = "The Pairs" a Matching/ Concentration game with the flashcards by matching the preterite with the imperfect. For example, **"Yo comí arroz con pollo"** would match with **"Yo comía arroz con pollo"** because the English is the same, "I ate chicken and rice." **Estudiar es un buen idea.** = To study is a good idea.

JUEGO DE "LAS PAREJAS" = GAME OF "THE PAIRS"

LECCIÓN 5
54 CINCUENTA Y CUATRO

Descriptives, comparatives and superlatives can take your Spanish sentences to the next level. Complete these sentences using the adjectives. Remember that many times the Spanish speaker will say what it is (noun) and then describe it (adjective).

GRAMÁTICA = GRAMMAR

Adjectivos = Adjectives (Descriptive and Comparative)

- Descriptive adjectives usually follow the noun that they describe and match the masculine, feminine or plural.
  For example: **la casa blanca, las casas blancas, el zapato blanco, los zapatos blancos.**

- Comparatives have an adjective in the middle: **más...que** = more...(adjective)...than
  menos...que = less...(adjective)...than
  tal...como = as...(adjective)...as

- Note that "**bueno**" = good is the adjective while "**bien**" = well is an adverb.
  Also "**mucho**" = a lot is an adjective while "**muy**" = very is an adverb.
  The words "**poco**" = a little and "**pequeño**" = small are both adjectives.

ADJECTIVO = ADJECTIVE	OPUESTOS = OPPOSITES	COLORES = COLORS
grande(s) = large	**pequeña(o)/s** = small	**blanca(o)/s** = white
mucha(o)/s = a lot	**poca(o)/s** = a little	**roja(o)/s** = red
buena(o)/s = good	**mala(o)/s** = bad	**azul(es)** = blue
mejor(es) = better	**peor(es)** = worse	**amarilla(o)/s** = yellow
mayor(es) = greater/older	**menor(es)** = less/younger	**negra(o)/s** = black
demasiada(o)/s = too much	**bastante** = enough	**anaranjada(o)/s** = orange

1. En la fiesta yo comí _____ comida. = At the party, I ate <u>a lot</u> of food.

2. Normalmente yo comía _____ ensalada. = Normally I used to eat a <u>little</u> salad.

3. Cuando yo tenía trece años, yo vivía lejos de las escuelas _____ . =
When I was thirteen years old, I used to live far from the <u>big</u> schools.

4. Yo viví cerca de la escuela _____ . = I lived the close to the <u>small</u> school.

5. Usted siempre quería un perro _____ . = You always used to want a <u>white</u> dog.

6. Él nunca quiso una gata _____ . = He never wanted a (female) <u>black</u> cat.

7. Mi abuelo tuvo dos hermanas _____ . = My grandpa had two <u>older</u> sisters.

8. Mi abuela tuvo un hermano _____ . = My grandma had a <u>younger</u> brother.

Guess which two sentences are **cierto** = true and which one is **falso** = false for the **Lugares para visitar** = Places to visit, and then do the same for the **Días festivos** = Holidays. Take a group vote by holding up either one, two or three fingers to show which one you believe is false. Use the Answer Key to find out why.

CULTURA = CULTURE

AMÉRICA DEL SUR = SOUTH AMERICA

CHILE | ARGENTINA | URUGUAY | PARAGUAY

Lugares para visitar en América del Sur = Places to visit in South America

(C | F) 1. Entre los años 1200 y 1500, La Isla de Pascua, al oeste de Chile tuvo más de 800 estatuas "Moai Moai" que pesaban entre 13 y 80 toneladas. Hoy en día todavía se puede ver casi la mitad de estas. =
Between the years of 1200 and 1500, Easter Island, west of Chile had more than 800 "Moai Moai" statues that weighed between 13 and 80 tons. Today you can still see almost half of these (statues).

(C | F) 2. Los turistas quisieron ver las 275 saltos de las cataratas de Iguazú cerca de las fronteras de Argentina, Paraguay y Brasil. Querían escuchar el agua de la "Garganta del Diablo." =
The tourists wanted to see the 275 falls of the Iguazú waterfalls near the borders of Argentina, Paraguay and Brazil. They wanted to hear the water at the "Devil's Throat."

(C | F) 3. En Colonia del Sacramento, Uruguay, los españoles vivieron felizmente en 1880 cuando comían empanadas y mate. =
In Colonia del Sacramento, Uruguay, the Spaniards lived happily in 1880 when they ate empanadas and mate.

Días festivos en América del Sur = Holidays in South America

(C | F) 1. Las personas que vivieron en las Américas en 1492 posiblemente conocieron a Cristóbal Colón. Hoy en día, llaman al 12 de octubre "El Día de la Raza." En Argentina, se llama "El Día del Respeto a la Diversidad Cultural." En Chile, se llama "El Día del Encuentro de Dos Mundos." Pero en Uruguay, se celebra el "El Día de las Américas" el 12 de abril. =
The people that lived in the Americas in 1492 possibly met Christopher Columbus. Nowadays, they call October 12 "The Day of the Race." In Argentina, they call it "The Day of Respect of Cultural Diversity." In Chile, they call it "The Day of Encounter (Discovery) of Two Worlds." But in Uruguay, they celebrate "The Day of the Americas" on April 12.

(C | F) 2. Ella siempre quería recordar el primer día de mayo, cuando celebraban "El Día del Maestro", "El Día del Niño" y "El Día Internacional de los Trabajadores" en muchos países de América del Sur. =
She always wanted to remember the first day of May when they celebrated the Teachers' Day, the Children's Day and the International Workers' Day in many South American countries.

(C | F) 3. En Argentina la gente celebraba la Navidad durante el verano, así por eso tenían pesebres y árboles con bolitas de algodón en lugar de nieve. Ellos tomaban sidra, comían panettone y carne a la parrilla. =
In Argentina, the people (have always) celebrated Christmas during summer, so that is why they made nativities and trees with cotton balls in place of snow. They (have always) drank alcoholic cider, ate Italian fruitcake (sweet bread) and grilled meat.

LECCIÓN 5
56 CINCUENTA Y SEIS

Here are some sentence starters using the verbs from the past two chapters. Write two true sentences and one false sentence about yourself and then read them in any order. We will vote to guess which one is false. Be creative and use things other people don't know about you. Use your imagination to complete these sentences.
Es muy divertido. = It is very fun.

TEMAS PARA CONVERSAR = CONVERSATIONAL TOPICS

2 cierto y 1 falso = 2 true and 1 false

IDEAS PARA LAS FRASES	SENTENCE IDEAS
SPANISH	ENGLISH
1. Una vez yo hablé con...	One time I spoke with... (someone famous?)
2. Yo trabajé como...	I worked as... (fun, interesting job we may not expect?)
3. Yo terminé...	I finished... (an interesting project, a difficult class?)
4. Yo empecé...	I began... (maybe you tried this once?)
5. Yo comí...	I ate... (a cultural experience?)
6. Yo viví...	I lived... (somewhere exotic? somewhere besides here?)
7. Yo tuve...	I had... (animals or pets? a great experience?)
8. Yo quise...	I wanted... (always wished for? a dream?)

TRACK 16

Your homework is to finish the next two pages. Keep an eye out for any current events in the news this week about South America. For this activity you will be doing two things. First finish the sentence in Spanish and then write the English equivalent for the entire sentence.

LECCIÓN 5

57 CINCUENTA Y SIETE

TAREA = HOMEWORK

1. Ayer yo comí... _____

2. Yo comía mucho... _____

3. Antes de ayer ella comió... _____

4. Él siempre vivía en... _____

5. Hace muchos años yo viví en... _____

6. En el pasado usted vivió con... _____

7. Hace 10 años yo tuve... _____

8. Usualmente yo tenía... _____

9. Generalmente ustedes tenían... _____

10. Yo todo el tiempo quería... _____

11. La semana pasada yo quise... _____

12. El otro día usted quiso... _____

LECCIÓN 5

58 CINCUENTA Y OCHO

Now you have an opportunity to practice. Conjugate each verb in Spanish and write it on the line provided. Next find these Spanish verbs in the word search. **¡Claro que sí!** = Of course!

UN POCO MÁS DE TAREA = A LITTLE MORE HOMEWORK

```
E I L A T A N C O R C Ó M D N
C O M I E R O N A T O E I C O
B E S I U Q O B Í I M A C O R
D I Í E M M V S I Á Í E H N E
A D N T N E I I Ó S E T E T I
B Í O G O O N Y V I R A E A V
A N R L R V E A N I C L L B I
G J E D E R M I M O Ó D C A V
U S I I I E L E N A R O S E D
J Í V E S V O L V Í E V U T Í
B J U L I A E L I A N A B V N
R A T E U O R D O R O N I D E
A D M N Q C N V D S M V M M D
D E S O M A U T N Q U I S O N
A N U L A T X A N Ó I M O C X
```

BUSCAPALABRAS = WORD SEARCH

(Note: these verbs are all in preterite past tense.)

1. he lived = **él** _____
2. I had = = **yo** _____
3. they wanted = **ellos** _____
4. you all ate = **ustedes** _____
5. she wanted = **ella** _____
6. I lived = **yo** _____
7. you had = **usted** _____
8. I ate = **yo** _____
9. I wanted = **yo** _____
10. he ate = **él** _____
11. they had = **ellos** _____
12. you all lived = **ustedes** _____

SPANISH CHATBOOK ❷ © SPANISH CHAT COMPANY

LECCIÓN 5

59 CINCUENTA Y NUEVE

Give this rubric to your teacher next time to use to evaluate your final project. Final projects were described on page 33 = **treinta y tres. Felicidades.** = Best wishes.

EVALUACIÓN DE SU PROYECTO FINAL = FINAL PROJECT EVALUATION

CALIDAD = QUALITY (NEATNESS)
Presentation quality work

CORRECTO = CORRECT SPANISH
Correct grammar, verbs, sentences and accent marks

CREATIVIDAD = CREATIVITY
Color, Visuals and Interesting project design

PRESENTACIÓN = PRESENTATION
Loud, Clear five minute demonstration of your project

ÚTIL = USEFUL / RELEVANT
Applicable to your job and your life

VERSIÓN INICIAL = ROUGH DRAFT
Rough draft edited by either a Spanish teacher or a fluent Spanish-speaker

A TIEMPO = ON TIME
Ready at the beginning of class

TOTAL
Total percentage score out of 100

LECCIÓN 6 LESSON

TERMINAMOS CHARLANDO. =

We finish chatting.

Los Verbos en la Lección 6 son:

ir = to go

ver = to see

estar = to be (changing)

ser = to be (permanent)

LECCIÓN 6
60 SESENTA

Begin by presenting your final projects explained on page 33 = **treinta y tres**. Now use these PAST TENSE **rule breaker** verbs as conversation starters for the entire group. Student #1 asks the first question and Student #2 answers. Now Student #2 asks the first question and Student #3 answers. Continue until everyone has asked and answered the first question. Then move on to the next question.

EMPIEZA AQUÍ = START HERE

1. VER = TO SEE
TENSE: PRETERITE PAST RULE BREAKER VERB

"¿Vio usted a alguien famoso alguna vez?"
(¿Vee-oh Oo-stehd Ah Ahl-gee/ehn Fah-moh-soh Ahl-goo-nah Vehs?)
Did you ever see someone famous?

"Una vez yo vi al presidente."
(Oo-nah Vehs Yoh Vee Ahl Preh-see-dehn-teh.)
One time I saw the president.

2. IR = TO GO
TENSE: PRETERITE PAST RULE BREAKER VERB
NOTE THAT SER IS ALSO "FUE & FUI" IN THE PAST TENSE- FIND EXAMPLES ON PAGE 62.

"¿A dónde fue para su última cita?"
(¿Ah DOHN-deh Foo/eh Pah-rah Soo OOL-tee-mah See-tah?)
Where did you go for your last date (or appointment)?

"Para mi última cita, yo fui al cine."
(Pah-rah Mee OOL-tee-mah See-tah Yoh Foo/ee Ahl See-neh.)
For my last appointment (or date), I went to the movie theater.

LUGARES = PLACES	
dentista = dentist	**película** = movie
doctor(a) = doctor	**restaurante** = restaurant
reunión = meeting/reunion	**bailar** = (to) dance
entrevista = interview	**un lugar especial** = a special place

TRACK 17

SPANISH CHATBOOK 2 © SPANISH CHAT COMPANY

This activity will be completed with partners. These three sentences use IMPERFECT PAST TENSE **rule breaker** verbs. You and your partner will do these final three conversation starters. **Fantástico.** = Fantastic.

LECCIÓN 6
61 SESENTA Y UNO

CON MIS COMPAÑEROS = WITH MY COLLEAGUES

3. IR A = TO GO TO
TENSE: IMPERFECT PAST -ER VERB

"¿Iba usted a cambiar algo en su vida?"
(¿Ee-bah Oo-stehd Ah Kahm-bee/ahr Ahl-goh Ehn Soo Vee-dah?)
Were you going to change something in your life?

"Yo iba a cambiar mi trabajo."
(Yoh Ee-bah Ah Kahm-bee/ahr Mee Trah-bah-hoh.)
I was going to change my job.

4. ESTAR = TO BE
TENSE: IMPERFECT PAST RULE BREAKER VERB

"¿Estaba usted feliz durante el mes pasado? ¿Por qué?"
(¿Ehs-tah-bah Oo-stehd Feh-leez Doo-rahn-teh Ehl Mehs Pah-sah-doh?)(Por KEH?)
Were you happy during the last month?

"Sí, yo estaba feliz porque visité a mis abuelos."
(SEE, Yoh Ehs-tah-bah Feh-leez Por-keh Vee-see-TEH Ah Mees Ah-boo/eh-lohs.)
Yes, I was happy because I visited my grandparents.

5. SER = TO BE
TENSE: IMPERFECT PAST -ER VERB

"¿Cuál era su meta?"
(¿KWAHL Eh-rah Soo Meh-tah?)
What was your goal?

"Mi meta era escribir un libro."
(Mee Meh-tah Eh-rah Ehs-cree-beer Oon Lee-broh.)
My goal was to write a book.

LECCIÓN 6

How do these past tense verbs work? The most commonly used verbs are the ones that don't follow the rules. Write a question and answer for each rule-breaker verb. Remember to put the verb first when writing a question. See the question examples from the charts on pages 12, 22 & 32. The Answer Key has ideas to help you write your 4 questions and 4 answers. Page 49 has clue words for Preterite vs. Imperfect. After you write them, practice with a partner. Note that ir and ser are the same in preterite.

YO SÉ LOS VERBOS = I KNOW THE VERBS

IDEAS PARA LAS FRASES = IDEAS FOR SENTENCES

IR* = went / used to go
memorize- this one breaks all the rules

- **P** Yo fui
- **I** Yo iba
- **P** Usted fue
- **I** Usted iba
- **P** Ustedes fueron
- **I** Ustedes iban

VER* = saw / used to see
preterite -no accent marks

- **P** Yo vi
- **I** Yo veía
- **P** Ella vio
- **I** Ella veía
- **P** Ellos v<u>ieron</u>
- **I** Ellos veían

ESTAR* = was / used to be (changing)
preterite -stem changes to -uv, the yo form has an e and there are no accents

- **P** Yo estuve
- **I** Yo est<u>aba</u>
- **P** Él estuvo
- **I** Él est<u>aba</u>
- **P** Gonzalo y Melissa estuv<u>ieron</u>
- **I** Gonzalo y Melissa est<u>aban</u>

SER* = was / used to be (permanent)
memorize- this one breaks all the rules

- **P** Yo fui
- **I** Yo era
- **P** Indira fue
- **I** Indira era
- **P** Rosa y Santiago fueron
- **I** Rose y James er<u>an</u>

P = Preterite
I = Imperfect

Cut these flashcards apart. To study your flashcards you will change the verb in each sentence from preterite to imperfect. Remember that preterite is over and done with while imperfect is continued or involved emotions. Get your flashcards out every morning for ten minutes and use them to review.

Recorta = Cut out along the dashed lines

YO VI AL DOCTOR. = I saw the doctor. *PRETERITE LECCIÓN 6*	**¿VIO USTED A ALGUIEN?** = Did you see anyone? *PRETERITE LECCIÓN 6*	**USTEDES VIERON EL PARTIDO.** = You all saw the game. *PRETERITE LECCIÓN 6*
YO FUI JUGADOR(A) DE BALONCESTO. = I was a basketball player. *PRETERITE LECCIÓN 6*	**¿FUE USTED JUGADOR(A) DE UN DEPORTE?** = Were you a player of a sport?. *PRETERITE LECCIÓN 6*	**ELLOS FUERON LOS DUEÑOS.** = They were the owners. *PRETERITE LECCIÓN 6*
YO FUI A UNA CITA. = I went to an appointment. *PRETERITE LECCIÓN 6*	**¿FUE USTED A UNA CITA?** = Did you go to an appointment? *PRETERITE LECCIÓN 6*	**ELLOS FUERON A LA IGLESIA.** = They went to church. *PRETERITE LECCIÓN 6*
YO ESTUVE FELIZ. = I was happy. *PRETERITE LECCIÓN 6*	**¿ESTUVO USTED FELIZ?** = Were you happy? *PRETERITE LECCIÓN 6*	**ELLOS ESTUVIERON SALUDABLES.** = They were healthy. *PRETERITE LECCIÓN 6*

© SPANISH CHAT COMPANY

SPANISH CHATBOOK ❷

USTEDES VEÍAN EL PARTIDO. = You all saw the game. IMPERFECT LECCIÓN 6	**¿VEÍA USTED A ALGUIEN?** = Did you see anyone? IMPERFECT LECCIÓN 6	**YO VEÍA AL DOCTOR.** = I saw the doctor. IMPERFECT LECCIÓN 6
ELLOS ERAN LOS DUEÑOS. = They were the owners. IMPERFECT LECCIÓN 6	**¿ERA USTED JUGADOR(A) DE UN DEPORTE?** = Were you a player of a sport? IMPERFECT LECCIÓN 6	**YO ERA JUGADOR(A) DE BALONCESTO.** = I was a basketball player. IMPERFECT LECCIÓN 6
ELLOS IBAN A LA IGLESIA. = They went to church. IMPERFECT LECCIÓN 6	**¿IBA USTED A UNA CITA?** = Did you go to an appointment? IMPERFECT LECCIÓN 6	**YO IBA A UNA CITA.** = I was going to an appointment. IMPERFECT LECCIÓN 6
ELLOS ESTABAN SALUDABLES. = They were healthy. IMPERFECT LECCIÓN 6	**¿ESTABA USTED FELIZ?** = Were you happy? IMPERFECT LECCIÓN 6	**YO ESTABA FELIZ.** = I was happy. IMPERFECT LECCIÓN 6

Play the "**Lotería** = Bingo" game. Select any 16 past tense flashcards from Lessons 4-6 and put them in four rows of four onto your desk or table, like the sample design below. Use the Past tense verb charts from p. 66 = **sesenta y seis** to call out the verbs in any order. Cover the squares with small pieces of paper or dried beans. Yell "**¡LOTERÍA!**" if you have four in a row. Note: **Lotería** also means "lottery" in some countries. Street vendors often sell the tickets.

LECCIÓN 6

63 SESENTA Y TRES

EL JUEGO DE "LOTERÍA" = THE GAME OF "BINGO"

LECCIÓN 6

64 SESENTA Y CUATRO

Prepositions connect a noun or a pronoun to another word in the sentence. Complete these sentences using the prepositions. The more you use Spanish, the more comfortable you will get with the prepositions. Don't give up, just keep chatting in Spanish and you will improve

GRAMÁTICA = GRAMMAR

Preposiciones = Prepositions

- Prepositions connect a pronoun or a noun to another word in the sentence.
- Use **"para"** when describing where someone is going, a purpose, an opinion and a deadline.

  Use **"por"** when describing a time of day or duration of time, a price, transportation or movement and a reason for something.

PREPOSICIONES = PREPOSITIONS		
a = to, at, on	**desde** = since, from	**hasta** = until, up to, as far as
alrededor = around	**después de** = after	**lejos** = far
antes de = before	**durante** = during	**para** = for, in order to
bajo = below, under	**en** = in, at, on	**por** = for, because of, by
cerca de = near/close to	**encima de** = on top of	**sin** = without
con = with	**entre** = between, among	**sobre** = above, on
de = of, from	**hacia** = toward	**tras** = behind

1. Llovió _____ de mi casa. = It rained <u>close</u> to my house.

2. Nevó _____ de mi apartamento. = It snowed <u>far</u> from my apartment.

3. El sol salió _____ mi patio y su jardín. = The sun came out <u>between</u> my patio and your garden.

4. Yo estuve _____ ella _____ la tormenta. = I was <u>with</u> her <u>during</u> the storm.

5. Estaba nublado cada día esta semana _____ ayer. = It was cloudy every day this week <u>until</u> yesterday.

Guess which two sentences are cierto = true and which one is falso = false for the Lugares para visitar = Places to visit, and then do the same for the Días festivos = Holidays. Take a group vote by holding up either one, two or three fingers to show which one you believe is false. Use the Answer Key to find out why.

LECCIÓN 6

CULTURA = CULTURE

LAS ISLAS Y ÁFRICA = THE ISLANDS AND AFRICA

PUERTO RICO | LA REPÚBLICA DOMINICANA | CUBA | GUINEA EQUATORIAL

Lugares para visitar en las islas y África = Places to visit in the islands and Africa

C | F) 1. El Rey Felipe II estuvo en El Castillo San Felipe del Morro de San Juan, Puerto Rico. Los Tres Reyes estuvieron en el Morro de La Habana, Cuba. Don Diego Colón, el hijo de Cristóbal estuvo en el Morro de Santo Domingo, República Dominicana. =
King Phillip II was in the fortress of San Juan, Puerto Rico. The Three Kings were in the fortress of Havana, Cuba. Sir Diego Columbus, the son of Christopher was in the fortress of Santo Domingo, Dominican Republic.

C | F) 2. En Guinea Equatorial, los turistas vieron más de 100 especies de cocodrilos, pájaros, mariposas y mamíferos (elefantes, monos y gorilas) en el Parque Nacional Monte Alén. =
In Equatorial Guinea, the tourists saw more than 100 species of crocodiles, birds, butterflies and mammals (elephants, monkeys and gorillas), in the Mt. Alén National Park.

C | F) 3. En mis viajes yo vi que la gente iba a lugares para bailar Merengue y Bachata en La República Dominicana; Mambo y Salsa en Cuba; y Reggaeton en Puerto Rico. =
In my travels, I saw people that went to places to dance the Merengue and Bachata in the Dominican Republic; Mambo and Salsa in Cuba; and "Reggaeton" in Puerto Rico.

Días festivos en las islas y África = Holidays in the islands and Africa

C | F) 1. En muchos países Latinoamericanos el día más feliz cada año para los niños siempre era el seis de enero, cuando veían sus zapatos llenos de dulces y regalos de parte de los Reyes Magos. =
In many Latin American countries the happiest day each year for kids always was January 6 when they saw their shoes full of sweets and gifts from the Magi Kings.

C | F) 2. El 25 de mayo es el "Día de África." Lo fue cuando los miembros de Guinea Equatorial y otros 52 estados declararon la importancia de la paz y la unidad de África. =
May 25 is the "Day of Africa." It was when the members of Equatorial Guinea and 52 other states declared the importance of the peace and unity of Africa.

C | F) 3. El primero de enero de 1959, fue el "Triunfo de la Revolución" y desde entonces, cada cuatro años, los ciudadanos iban a votar por su candidato favorito. =
January 1, 1959, was the "Triumph of the Revolution" and since then, every four years, the citizens go to vote for their favorite canditate.

LECCIÓN 6

66 SESENTA Y SEIS

Write your own three questions using this chart of all of the Imperfect and Preterite past tense verbs found in this book. Share these by asking someone your three questions and answering their questions. Then switch partners as time allows.

TEMAS PARA CONVERSAR = CONVERSATIONAL TOPICS

INFINITIVE FORM TO...	EMPEZAR	TERMINAR	HABLAR	TRABAJAR	COMER	QUERER	TENER	VIVIR	IR	VER	ESTAR	SER
PRETERITE YO = I	yo empecé	yo terminé	yo hablé	yo trabajé	yo comí	yo quise	yo tuve	yo viví	yo fui	yo vi	yo estuve	yo fui
PRETERITE ELLA, ÉL, USTED = ONE SUBJECT	ella empezó	él terminó	usted habló	Mónica trabajó	ella comió	él quiso	usted tuvo	Santiago vivió	ella fue	él vio	usted estuvo	Zorro fue
PRETERITE USTEDES/ ELLOS = YOU PLURAL/ THEY	ellos empezaron	ustedes terminaron	María y José hablaron	ellos trabajaron	La Señora y el Señor comieron	ellos quisieron	ustedes tuvieron	Carolina y su esposo vivieron	ellos fueron	ustedes vieron	Luisa y Teresa estuvieron	ellos fueron
IMPERFECT YO = I	yo empezaba	yo terminaba	yo hablaba	yo trabajaba	yo comía	yo quería	yo tenía	yo vivía	yo iba	yo veía	yo estaba	yo era
IMPERFECT ELLA, ÉL, USTED = ONE SUBJECT	ella empezaba	él terminaba	usted hablaba	Lorena trabajaba	ella comía	él quería	usted tenía	Susana vivía	ella iba	él veía	usted estaba	Eduardo era
IMPERFECT USTEDES/ ELLOS = YOU PLURAL/ THEY	ellos empezaban	ustedes terminaban	Catarina y Timoteo hablaban	ellos trabajaban	Alejandra y Miguel comían	ellos querían	ustedes tenían	Indira y Jefe vivían	ellos iban	ustedes veían	Luisa, Teresa y Juan estaban	ellos eran

SPANISH CHATBOOK 2 © SPANISH CHAT COMPANY

LECCIÓN 6

Your homework is to finish the next two pages. Keep an eye out for any current events in the news this week about the Spanish-speaking islands. For this activity you will be doing two things. First finish the sentence in Spanish and then write the English equivalent for the entire sentence. This could be used as a final exam.

TAREA O EXAMEN FINAL = HOMEWORK OR FINAL EXAM

1. Anoche yo vi... _____

2. Hace un mes ella vio... _____

3. Mientras ella no veía.. _____

4. Hace muchos años yo iba a... _____

5. De vez en cuando él iba a... _____

6. Ayer por la tarde usted fue... _____

7. En ese momento usted estuvo.. y entonces... _____

8. Con frecuencia usted estaba... _____

9. A veces ustedes estaban... _____

10. Todos los días yo era... _____

11. Durante el año pasado yo fui... _____

12. Hace un mes ellos fueron... _____

LECCIÓN 6

68 SESENTA Y OCHO

This can be done as homework. Complete the "Secret word puzzle" by using the correct verb conjugations. The Spanish verb will fit in the boxes exactly if it is correct. **Gracias por su trabajo durante la clase de español.** = Thank you for your work during the Spanish class.

1 you were (ser / preterite) =
usted _____

2 she went (ir / imperfect) =
ella _____

3 they saw (ver / imperfect) =
(all females) ellas _____

4 I was (estar / preterite) =
yo _____

5 he was (ser / imperfect) =
él _____
(Add an accent mark for the secret word below)

6 I was (estar / imperfect) =
él _____

7 they were (estar / preterite) =
ellos _____

8 I went (ir / preterite) =
yo _____

9 you all ate (comer / imperfect)
ustedes _____

10 you saw (ver / preterite) =
usted _____

1 2 3 4 5 6 7 8 9 10

SPANISH CHATBOOK 2   © SPANISH CHAT COMPANY

LECCIÓN 6

69 SESENTA Y NUEVE

Here are 10 ideas that will help you to continue learning Spanish. The most important thing is to find opportunities to practice.

AYÚDAME POR FAVOR = HELP ME PLEASE

1. **Juego** = Game: Invent your own board game that practices Spanish vocabulary and phrases. You could also make a matching game or any of the other games from the six lessons. Create a crucigrama = crossword puzzle or buscapalabras = word search and give it to your friends to practice.

2. **Tarjetas** = Flashcards: Make new flashcards with other vocabulary words such as animals, body parts or more food words. Learn a new phrase each and every day. Play some of the games from the *Spanish Chatbook 2* using your new flashcards.

3. **Mantel Individual o Cartel** = Place mat or poster: Decorate and design your project with lots of Spanish vocabulary and phrases. Laminate it with clear contact paper to make it more durable.

4. **Vídeo Casero** = Home video: Practice a skit in Spanish and then record a movie. Make puppets or recruit friends and family to be a part of your video. You could act out the story of the Three Bears or any other fairy tale. Look at Hispanic **Leyendas** = Folktales for other ideas. A cooking show would also be fun to record. Tell about the ingredients and give directions in Spanish. Take the viewer on a tour of your home or city in Spanish. Try to sell a product with a Spanish infomercial. There are many possibilities so invent your own idea for a movie in Spanish. Have a native speaker review the script.

5. **Menú** = Menu: Design your own Spanish menu and describe each item that you are serving. Research menus for ideas. Use the recipes as guides on pages #70-72 = setenta hasta setenta y dos.

6. **Estudia** = Study: Use the Extra Grammar guide and exercises from the back of the book to practice and study the Spanish language. Attend a class at your local university or online. Try another *Spanish Chatbook* class, find out more about our *Business Spanish Chatbook, Culinary Spanish Chatbook, Elementary Spanish Chatbook* and *Spanish Chatbook* at our web site, SpanishChatCompany.com.

7. **Habla** = Talk: Create opportunities for speaking Spanish. Ask native speakers questions in Spanish and learn more responses. Practice a new phrase each and every day.

8. **Cultura** = Culture: There is a lot of diversity in the Spanish-speaking world. Find Hispanic cultural activities nearby or spend a week at a language school in Latin America.

9. **Almuerzo** = Lunch: Plan a specific day to speak Spanish or have a monthly luncheon led by a Spanish speaker. Discuss current events, your interests or what is happening in you life. Use the flashcards and activities from this book to ask questions in Spanish. Use the recipes from #70-72 to add some Latin flavor.

10. **¡Inténtelo!** = Try it!: Try out your new skills and continue to comunicate in Spanish. Finally, remember "**Donde existe voluntad, hay un camino.** = Where there is a will, there is a way."

SU OPINIÓN, POR FAVOR = YOUR OPINION, PLEASE

Use this feedback form to evaluate your learning.
Gracias = Thank you for your honest feedback.
You may also submit feedback at our web site SpanishChatCompany.com

1. What phrases will you use the most? _____
   _____
   _____
   _____

2. What three activities helped you the most? _____
   _____
   _____
   _____

3. What cultural considerations will help you? _____
   _____
   _____
   _____

4. What would you like to do differently next time you study Spanish?
   _____
   _____
   _____

5. What would you still like to learn? _____
   _____
   _____
   _____

6. Any further questions or comments? _____
   _____
   _____
   _____

Recorta = Cut out along the dashed lines

SPANISH CHATBOOK

CERTIFICADO DE RECONOCIMIENTO

Me llamo: _____

La fecha es el _____ de la maestra o el maestro _____

LEARN SPANISH TODAY FOR WORK & PLAY

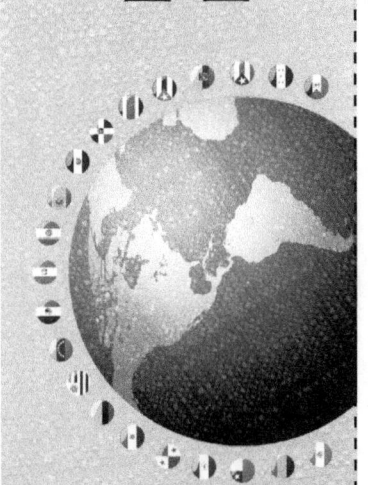

APENDICÉ  APPENDIX

AL FINAL =
At the end

Las Páginas son:
The Pages are:

Recetas & Días Festivos =
Recipes & Holidays

Gramática = Extra grammar including accent marks and regular & irregular verb conjugation

Glosario = glossary of the vocabulary used in this book: English = Spanish & Español = Inglés

60 verbos = 60 verbs in present, preterite & imperfect tenses

AL FINAL — RECETAS = RECIPES

1. **TORTILLA DE PATATAS (SPAIN):** A Tortilla de patatas is made with 2 onions, 4 potatoes and 6 eggs. Heat olive oil in a deep fat fryer. This can also be done in a skillet. Heat enough olive oil to cover the potatoes; this may be a cup or more of oil. Cut the potatoes and onions into small (1/2 inch) slices and fry them until brown. Lightly salt them to taste. In a separate bowl, stir the eggs a few times without beating them. Add the potatoes/onions to the eggs. Heat 1 tablespoon of olive oil in a skillet and add the egg/potato/onions mixture. Cook on medium heat for about 10 minutes. Top the skillet with a plate and flip it over. Heat 1 tablespoon of olive oil in the skillet and slide the "tortilla de patatas" back into the pan. Heat for about 5–10 minutes. Eat hot or cold. In Spain they use long baguette bread and put the "tortilla de patatas" inside as a sandwich. You will find one triangle piece of tortilla de patatas as a typical tapas dish.

2. **TORTILLAS/PUPUSAS/AREPAS (LATIN AMERICA):** It is easy to make your own tortillas. Buy "harina preparada para las tortillas" (tortilla flour). Take either the corn or white tortilla flour and then add the water and salt according to the package. Roll a ball and then shape them with a tortilla press. If you don't have a tortilla press, push a plate down onto the dough to cut a circle or press the tortilla into a circle with your hands. Hint: You may want to use wax paper on each side of the dough ball to prevent it from sticking to the tortilla press. Finally, cook the tortilla on an electric skillet or pancake griddle for just a few minutes on each side. Finally, sprinkle them with cinnamon and sugar or top with salsa and cheese. To make pupusas or arepas follow the same steps, but make the dough thicker. ¡Qué rico! = How tasty!

3. **GALLO PINTO (COSTA RICA):** In Nicaragua and Honduras, Gallo Pinto is usually made with red beans, whereas in Costa Rica, it is made with black beans. To make Gallo Pinto, heat 1 tablespoon of olive oil in a skillet. Sauté 1 chopped white onion and 2 cloves of garlic. Stir in one can of cooked black beans. (Do not drain.) Add 2 cups of cooked white rice and 1 teaspoon of Worcestershire sauce to the bean mix, and simmer for 5–10 minutes. Add a dash or two of crushed red pepper to taste. Chop some fresh cilantro and add that to the Gallo Pinto, but be careful because a small amount is very flavorful. Heat the mixture thoroughly and serve for breakfast with scrambled eggs.

4. **SOPAPILLAS (MÉXICO):** Mix together 1 teaspoon of salt, 2 teaspoons baking powder and 4 cups flour. Cut in 4 tablespoons of shortening. Measure 1 1/2 cups warm water and add to the dry ingredients. Mix the dough until it is smooth. Cover and let the dough rest for 20 minutes. Next, sprinkle flour onto a board and roll the dough until it is about 1/4 inch thick. Cut the dough into squares of about 3 inches. Add 2 quarts oil into a deep-fat fryer and heat to 375 degrees F. Use a candy thermometer to check that the oil is exactly 375 degrees so the sopapillas will puff up. Fry until golden brown, flipping them over halfway through. Put them on a plate with paper towels. Sprinkle with cinnamon and sugar. Serve them warm. Remember to reheat the oil to 375 between batches. This recipe makes about 2 dozen.

RECETAS = RECIPES

AL FINAL

5. **CUBAN SANDWICHES (CUBA):** Slice one loaf of Cuban, Italian, or French bread into 4 parts. Split each part in half so that it is ready to fill. Spread mayonnaise or mustard on the bottom part of the bread. Stack the bread with sliced ham, roast pork, thin dill pickle slices and slices of Swiss cheese. Now add the top half of the bread. Brush with olive oil or butter. Put a heavy skillet on top of the sandwiches before grilling or baking in the oven. This will press them flat. Use a sandwich press for the same results. Bake them in the oven at 350 degrees until the cheese is melted.

6. **QUESADILLAS (MÉXICO):** Quesadillas are easy to make with a quesadilla maker or by folding one tortilla in half and cooking it on a sandwich-type grill. With a quesadilla maker, use two burrito-sized flour tortilla shells and fill them with your favorite meats and cheeses. Add salsa, black beans, corn and other spices. For a twist, make sweet, dessert quesadillas by adding cooked apples or slices of banana, cinnamon, and brown sugar to the plain tortillas and then cooking them. Serve with vanilla ice cream or whipped cream.

7. **TOSTADAS (MÉXICO):** To make tostadas buy a package of tostada shells or fry your own. Spread with refried beans, then add chopped tomatoes and shredded lettuce. Top with Oaxacan or cheddar cheese, salsa and sliced avocados or any additional toppings as desired.

8. **ARROZ CON LECHE (SPAIN/LATIN AMERICA):** To make this rice pudding, boil 4 cups of water with cinnamon. Add 2 cups of minute rice and cover for 5 minutes. Follow the package directions for other types of rice. Combine the rice with one can of sweetened condensed milk, one can of evaporated milk, a splash of vanilla, a dash of nutmeg and raisins. Add more rice to make a thicker pudding. Refrigerate for 1 hour and sprinkle cinnamon on top before serving.

9. **CHICLE = CHEWING GUM (LATIN AMERICA):** Make your own chewing gum with a kit benefiting the chicleros in the rainforest. Chicleros are people who collect the sap from the chicle (gum) tree. Kits include the sap to melt and all of the ingredients. Kits to make your own gum can be found online.

10. **CHOCOLATE (SOUTH AMERICA):** Chocolate comes from the cocoa bean pod, which may be found in the rainforests of Central and South America. Many companies sell authentic Latin American chocolates on the Internet and in Hispanic grocery stores. Make your own chocolate lollipops by melting chocolate chips and pouring them into any candy mold. Add lollipop sticks and freeze for about 10 minute. Kits to make your own chocolate candies from scratch can be found online.

11. **CHOCOLATE CALIENTE = HOT CHOCOLATE (MÉXICO):** There are many different brands of Mexican Hot chocolate, such as "Ibarra" and "Abuelita." Blend the chocolate/cinnamon bark in the blender with hot milk to make a delicious drink in cold weather. Be sure to hold the top on the blender so the mixture doesn't fly out. Hot chocolate is even served for breakfast in Oaxaca, México.

AL FINAL — RECETAS = RECIPES

12. **TOSTONES (PUERTO RICO):** Tostones are fried plantains. The plantain looks like a huge banana, but it is really more like a potato so don't eat it raw. Heat 1/2 cup of oil in a skillet. Cut the plantain into circle slices. Fry the slices and then remove them from the skillet. Flatten them by smashing them with a plate or the bottom of a glass or use a "tostonera" from Puerto Rico. Dip the plantains in water, and then fry them again in the hot oil. Salt to taste and eat these while warm. Pre-packaged banana chips can be found in some grocery stores.

13. **QUESO FUNDIDO = CHEESE DIP (MÉXICO):** Cheese dip can be made by melting a processed block cheese and salsa together. Or use a can of tomatoes and add cooked ground beef or chorizo. For a more authentic queso dip use Oaxacan cheese or any other fresh Mexican cheese that melts really well. Serve with chips.

14. **CHURROS (SPAIN):** Churros resemble long cinnamon sugar breadsticks. The dough may be made by combining 2 cups biscuit mix and 1 and 3/4 cups hot water. Stir for a few minutes. Roll the dough into long tubes or squeeze through a pastry bag. Fry 2 at a time in a deep fat fryer and then roll in a mixture of cinnamon and sugar. Eat warm. Other authentic churro recipes can be found on the internet.

15. **FLAN (LATIN AMERICA):** To make flan, put 1 cup of sugar in a saucepan and stir constantly on medium/low heat until liquid. Quickly pour the "caramel" to the bottom of a 10-inch pie plate or flan mold. In a separate bowl, stir 3 large eggs lightly. Add 1 can of evaporated milk, 1 can of sweetened condensed milk and 1 tablespoon of vanilla to the eggs. Gently stir to mix, do not beat. Pour into the pie plate or mold. Use a double boiler or put about 1 inch of boiling water in a larger pan and put the pie plate inside. This is called a Baño María = Maria's bath. Bake at 325 degrees for approximately 45 minutes. Refrigerate overnight or at least 4 hours and then flip over onto a serving dish allowing the caramel to drizzle across the top. It may be easier to buy a package of flan mix and just add milk.

16. **ENCHILADAS (MÉXICO):** To make enchiladas, start by browning one pound of hamburger. Add 3 ounces of cream cheese, 1 cup of salsa, 1/2 tablespoon of cumin, and 1 cup of shredded fiesta cheese to the hamburger. Grease a 9x13 pan. Put 3 spoonfuls of the hamburger mixture in one burrito-size tortilla and roll it up. About 6 burritos will fit in the pan. Then cover with 1 jar of enchilada sauce. Top with the remaining 1 cup of fiesta cheese and bake uncovered at 350 degrees F for 40 minutes.

17. **SALSA (LATIN AMERICA):** In a blender or food processor, combine 2 chopped green onions and 1 diced clove of garlic. Add cilantro, crushed red pepper and salt to taste. Add 2 1/2 cups of tomatoes fresh from the garden. Blend for a few seconds and serve with blue corn tortilla chips.

18. **OTHER RECIPES:** You can find many other recipes in cookbooks or online.

¡BUEN PROVECHO! = ENJOY YOUR MEAL!

DÍAS FESTIVOS = HOLIDAYS

AL FINAL

73 SETENTA Y TRES

- **Año Nuevo y Nochevieja** = New Year and New Year's Eve is on January 1 and December 31. Many people eat 12 grapes as the clock strikes midnight. Wearing yellow underwear in Peru is a symbol of good luck, while wearing black can mean bad luck. Sweeping out the house symbolizes sweeping out the old; in Cuba, they also throw a bucket of water out the window. In South America, walking around the house or block with suitcases is supposed to help bring travel opportunities, while in Ecuador they hide money around the house. In Chile, they wait for the new year in a graveyard and eat lentils for good luck. In Panamá, Ecuador, Paraguay and Colombia, they make a scarecrow "muñeco" and burn it in a bonfire to symbolize getting rid of the past. Fireworks are common throughout Latin America. IDEA: Make a poster or act out a play with these traditions.

- **El Día de los Reyes Magos** = The Day of the Three Magi Kings is on January 6. Latino children place their shoes by the door before going to bed. While they sleep the Three Kings, "Melchor, Gaspar y Baltazar" come and leave a gift. Traditionally, children would only get gifts from the Kings and not for Christmas, but now they may get gifts for both holidays. The Rosca/Roscón de Reyes = Cake of the Kings / Panettone is a fruitcake eaten on this holiday. A coin or small plastic baby "Jesus" is often hidden inside the cake. The person that finds the baby has to host the next party. IDEA: Make a King's cake and give a crown to the student that finds the baby. Have students each put one shoe in the hallway and go back to the classroom. Recruit another teacher to put a piece of candy, a sticker, or a small gift inside each shoe.

- **Día de los Enamorados /Día de San Valentín / Día de Amor y la Amistad** = Valentine's Day is usually celebrated on February 14. Although, in Colombia, it is in September and Día de Amor y la Amistad = Day of Love and Friendship can also be celebrated in July. It is a day to honor loved ones with flowers, candies and cards. It is also popular to draw names for an "amigo secreto" = secret friend and anonymously give that person notes and gifts for a week IDEA: Draw names for an "amigo secreto" and make cards and notes in Spanish. Use some of the positive phrases from page 6 = seis.

- **Carnaval** = Carnival is a Mardi Gras which is usually in February or early March. In Puerto Rico, Cuba and the Dominican Republic, they make elaborate masks and parade to Conga and other Latin music. In Puerto Rico, folks dress as a "Vejigante" with brightly colored spotted outfits and masks with five or more horns. They carry a "veija" = dried, painted cow bladder filled with air like a balloon. Parades and parties often are held on Fat Tuesday which is the day before Ash Wednesday. In Spain, groups of friends coordinate costumes and dress up in themes. For example, they might all be witches, babies or soccer players. IDEA: Make Carnavales masks from the *Elementary Spanish Chatbook* and have a parade with Conga music. Have students tie a balloon onto a stick or make a maraca.

- **Semana Santa and Pascua** = Holy week and Easter is sometime in March or April. Some Latin Americans go to church every day for this week. Church bells are silenced on Good Friday. During processions in Sevilla, Spain, as many as 50 people carry "pasos" = wooden religious sculptures and others dress in robes of various colors with matching pointed hoods. In Copán, Honduras, they use sawdust and flowers to make colorful designs on the streets before the Good Friday parade. Typical foods are: Rosca de Pascua = Easter cake ring, Potaje de la Vigilia = Vigil fasting soup, Ceviche = raw lemon soaked fish, Tortas de Pescado = fish cakes. IDEA: Make Cascarones from the *Elementary Spanish Chatbook* and try some Latin American fish recipes.

DÍAS FESTIVOS = HOLIDAYS

- **Día de la Madre** = Mother's Day is celebrated the second Sunday in May in many countries. Although in Spain it is the first Sunday in May and in Paraguay it is always May 15, "Madre Patria" = Mother Nation. May 10 is always Mother's Day in Mexico and El Salvador. Costa Rica honors mothers on August 15 = Assumption of Mary. Panama celebrates on December 8 and Argentina has their Mother's Day in October. IDEA: Make a card in Spanish for your mom, aunt or grandma.

- **Día del Padre** = Father's Day is celebrated in many countries on the 3rd Sunday in June. In Bolivia, Honduras, Uruguay and Spain, it is combined with the Día de San José = Day of St. Joseph. In Argentina, it is August 24 and in Uruguay it is in July. IDEA: Make a card in Spanish for your dad, uncle or grandpa.

- **Día del Niño** = Children's Day is officially November 20 according to the United Nations and is celebrated in Spain on that day but other countries honor a different day. Children throughout Latin America receive a present for this special day and have special activities or even a day off school. In Mexico it is April 30; Bolivia is on April 12 while Colombia and Peru also celebrate in April. June 1 is Nicaragua and Ecuador although Venezuela, Cuba and Panama all honor their children with a special day sometime in July. Uruguay, Chile, Peru, Paraguay, Puerto Rico and Argentina all celebrate in August. September 9 is Children's Day in Costa Rica; September 10 is Honduras while October 1 is El Salvador and Guatemala. Finally, the Dominican Republic have their day for children in December. IDEA: Draw the flag of each country on the calendar and send positive thoughts to the children of that country on that day or do a service learning project to help a child on each Children's Day.

- **Día del Maestro** = Teacher's Day is celebrated on many different days. In Mexico, it is on May 15 although the dates vary throughout Latin America. IDEA: Make a Spanish card or bring flowers to your favorite teacher.

- **Cinco de Mayo** = May 5 is a celebration of the victory of one Mexican battle against the French in 1862. Cinco de Mayo is actually a bigger celebration in the United States, demonstrating Mexican-American pride. IDEA: Have a parade for Cinco de Mayo and ask everyone to wear red, white and green. Make serapes = scarves out of grocery sacks, make maracas and dance to the song from the Elementary Spanish Chatbook CD- "El Alfabeto."

- **Día de Independencía** = Independence Day is one of the biggest celebrations in each country, with parades and festivals in the town square. For example, Independence Day in México is September 16. (Many people confuse this with Cinco de Mayo.) Independence Day in Guatemala, El Salvador, Honduras, Nicaragua and Costa Rica is September 15. IDEA: Have a parade for Independence Day for a Spanish-speaking country and make flags and banners to represent the country that you have chosen.

DÍAS FESTIVOS = HOLIDAYS

AL FINAL 75 SETENTA Y CINCO

- **Día de la Hispanidad** = Day of the Hispanic world honors the discovery of the Américas on October 12, 1492, by explorers such as Cristóbal Colón = Christopher Columbus. The day is also called "Día de la Raza" = "Day of the Race." In Argentina they call it "Día del Respeto a la Diversidad Cultural" = "Day of Respect of Cultural Diversity." In Chile they call it "Día del Encuentro de Dos Mundos" = "Day of Encounter (Discovery) of 2 Worlds." In Uruguay, they celebrate "Día de las Américas" = "Day of the Americas" on April 12. IDEA: Have a potluck during Hispanic Heritage month and invite and interview Latinos in your community.

- **Día de Brujas** = Halloween on October 31 is not a traditional Latin American holiday. However, in some places such as Chile, Colombia and Mexico, children have been influenced by Hollywood and are starting to ask neighbors for candies by saying "Dulce o Truco" = "Sweet or Trick." In Costa Rica, some people now go to costume parties at the discos. It is also known as "Víspera del Día de Todos los Santos = Eve of All Saints' Day." IDEA: Make a skeleton by gluing pasta on black paper and label the body parts with a white crayon. Draw a haunted house and label the furniture and Halloween icons in Spanish. Did you know that Murciélago = bat is one of the only Spanish words that includes all of the vowels?

- **Día de los Muertos** = Day of the Dead is celebrated November 1–2 primarily in Mexico, but some other places in Latin America also honor their loved ones. This is essentially like Memorial Day. Families leave a trail of marigold flowers from their house to the cemetary in the hopes that the souls are able to find their way back home for one day. They build ofrendas = altars with sugar skulls to honor the deceased. IDEA: Try making your own ofrenda.

- **Día de Acción de Gracias** = Thanksgiving is celebrated in the United States of America and Canada on the fourth Thursday in November. This is not a Latin American holiday. IDEA: Translate a menu of your typical holiday dinner into Spanish. IDEA: Make a place mat with Spanish words & phrases.

- **Las Posadas** = The Inns is celebrated in Mexico, Guatemala and Colombia from December 16-24. The nine days before Christmas symbolize the nine months before Jesus' birth. Each family commemorates the occasion differently, but many times they will sing villancicos = traditional holiday songs and gather together for meals with friends and relatives. Some groups of neighbors knock on door after door and are turned away by each "innkeeper." At the final house, they are let in for the fiesta = party usually with a star piñata The process is repeated for nine nights in a row with a different family hosting each evening. IDEA: Make a piñata using a balloon. Papier-mâché it by dipping newspapers into a mixture of glue and water. Let it dry and paint it. Fill it with candy and hang it from a tree. Hit it with a stick to break it open saying, "dale, dale, dale." = "give it, give it, give it."

- **Nochebuena and Navidad** = Christmas Eve and Christmas Day is celebrated on December 24-25 throughout Latin America and Spain. Poinsettias are used as decorations. This is an important Christian holiday with celebrations at churches and family dinners. Usually the figure of the baby Jesus is not placed into the manger until Christmas Day. Papá Noel = Santa Claus brings gifts and you will see many lights and decorations. Puerto Rico celebrates from November until February. IDEA: Research the stories and legends of the Poinsettia flower. Make poinsettias out of construction paper and act out the story. Make a holiday card or gift for someone special.

EXTRA GRAMMAR: ACCENT MARKS

AL FINAL 76 *setenta y seis*

WHEN TO USE AN ACCENT:

Ask a native speaker to pronounce these words for you and circle where the emphasis or stress is heard.

- **CHECK #1** If a word ends in a vowel a-e-i-o-u or -n-s, the natural stress should be on the next to the last syllable. You do not need an accent mark. For example: **examen, abuelos, hijo, maestra, luces**

- **CHECK #2** If a word ends in any other consonant, then the natural stress should be on the last syllable. You do not need an accent mark. For example: **universidad, español, cultural, electricidad, medidor**

- **BINGO!** Any exception to #1 or #2 will have an accent mark on the stressed vowel.
  sábado miércoles José teléfono número adiós dirección

ON A MAC:

To type: á, é, í, ó, ú,
On a Mac, hold down these two keys at the same time; then the next letter you type will have an accent mark.
Note: If this does not work, use the help function for your computer.

[Option] [E]

To type: ¿
On a Mac, hold down all three of these keys at the same time. When you let go and the ¿ will appear

[Option] [Shift] [?]

To type: ¡
On a Mac, hold down these two keys at the same time. When you let go and the ¡ will appear.

[Option] [1]

To type: ñ
On a Mac, hold down these two keys at the same time; then type "n" or "N" and it will have a tilde.

[Option] [N]

EXTRA GRAMMAR: ACCENT MARKS

AL FINAL
77 SETENTA Y SIETE

ON A PC:

To type: á, é, í, ó, ú,
On a PC, hold down CTRL and '(apostrophe) at the same time; then the next letter you type will have an accent mark. *If this does not work, see another way below or search for help using your computer.*

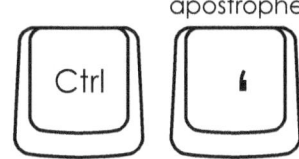

To type: ¿
On a PC, hold down all four of these keys at the same time.

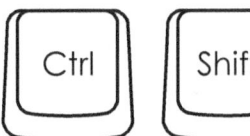   

To type: ¡
On a PC, hold down all four of these keys at the same time.

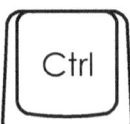  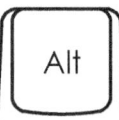 

To type: ñ
On a PC, hold down all three of these keys at the same time; then type "n" or "N" and it will have a tilde.

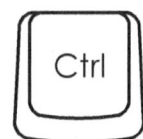 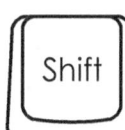 

LA PRÁCTICA = THE PRACTICE

Find a native speaker and listen to them pronounce these words. Put an accent mark where you hear the stress. When you are finished, check your answers in the Answer Key.

1. Ingles
2. bibliografia
3. ficcion
4. dolares
5. puerta
6. periodico

ANOTHER WAY TO MAKE ACCENT MARKS

Turn your NUM LOCK light on then hold down the ALT key while you type the numbers. When you let go of the keys the accented letter will appear:

- Hold down ALT and then type 160 to get á
- Hold down ALT and then type 130 to get é
- Hold down ALT and then type 161 to get í
- Hold down ALT and then type 162 to get ó
- Hold down ALT and then type 163 to get ú
- Hold down ALT and then type 164 to get ñ
- Hold down ALT and then type 168 to get ¿
- Hold down ALT and then type 0161 to get ¡

AL FINAL

EXTRA GRAMMAR: GUSTAR

TO LIKE = GUSTAR:

Gustar The verb gustar is also helpful in basic Spanish phrases. It means to be pleasing to someone. It's mainly used in the third person either singular or plural. When you use this verb, you need an indirect object pronoun.

Here are some examples of correct usage of gustar:

I like. = Me gusta (n)	We like.= Nos gusta (n)
You like. (informal, singular) = Te gusta (n)	You like. (plural, Spain) = Os gusta (n)
He likes. = Le gusta (n) She likes = Le gusta (n) You like. (formal, singular) = Le gusta (n)	They like. = Les gusta (n) You like. (formal, plural) = Les gusta (n)

I like to study. = Me gusta estudiar.
I like pizza. = Me gusta la pizza.
I like the books. = Me gustan los libros.
We like to work. = Nos gusta trabajar.
Do you like to study? = ¿Le gusta estudiar?
Renee, Chad, and Jude like to sleep. = A Reina, Carlos, y Judas, les gustan dormir.
David likes the computer. = A David, le gusta la computadora.

How would you translate these eight sentences?

1. She likes to swim. (to swim = nadar) _____

2. Do you like the book? _____

3. Mary and Bernard like to read. _____

4. He likes to fish. (to fish = pescar) _____

5. They like pizza. _____

6. I like the books. _____

7. You (plural) like to travel. (to travel = viajar) _____

8. We like to read Spanish. (to read= leer) _____

EXTRA GRAMMAR: INDIRECT/DIRECT OBJECT PRONOUNS

INDIRECT OBJECT PRONOUNS:

to me = me
to us = nos
to you (familiar) = te

to you (plural, Spain) = os
to him, to her, to you (formal) = le
to them, to you (plural, formal) = les

DIRECT OBJECT PRONOUNS:

me = me
us = nos
you (familiar) = te
you (plural, Spain) = os

him, it, you (masculine) = lo
her, it, you (feminine) = la
them, you (plural, masculine) = los
them, you (plural, feminine) = las

If you weren't paying attention in sixth-grade English class, it might be time for a little review. A pronoun is a word that replaces a noun. Let's start with a sentence in English. For example; Charlie throws the ball to Mary. Charlie is the subject of the sentence. Threw is the action word or verb. Ball would be the direct object. Mary is the indirect object.

Here is the same sentence in Spanish: Carlos tira la pelota a María. Carlos is the subject. Tira is the verb. Pelota is the direct object. María is the indirect object. Take this sentence and replace the direct and indirect objects with pronouns keeping in mind these three rules:

Rule #1: The pronouns have to agree with the word they're replacing.

Rule #2: When two pronouns are in one sentence, the indirect object comes before the direct object.

Rule #3: When le or les is followed by lo, la, los, or las, change the le or les to se.

Example #1: If you take the sentence (Carlos tira la pelota a María) and substitute the direct object for a pronoun, the new sentence would be the following: Carlos la tira a María. (Charlie threw it to Mary.) The direct object pronoun "la" replaces the word "pelota" and would be translated as it. (See Rule #1)

Example #2: If you substitute the indirect object with a pronoun, the new sentence would read: Carlos le tira la pelota. (Charlie threw the ball to her.) The indirect object pronoun "le" replaces the word "a María."

Example #3: Now if you replace both the direct and indirect objects with pronouns the new sentence would read: "Carlos se la tira." (Charlie threw it to her.) The "se" refers to Mary. The "la" refers to the ball. Originally it would be Carlos le la tira, but we have to change it to Carlos se la tira because of Rule #3.

For future reference, remember pronouns can be placed before any verb. Pronouns can go either before or after these three types of verbs:

1. an infinitive which is a verb that is not conjugated
2. a verb ending in –ando or –iendo This is the equivalent of –ing in Spanish.
3. affirmative commands

EXTRA GRAMMAR: REFLEXIVE / PRESENT PROGRESSIVE

REFLEXIVE

When people perform an action that reflects back onto them, in Spanish use reflexive verbs. In the dictionary you might see the reflexive pronoun –se attached to the verb. For example, you might see the verbs lavar and lavarse. Lavar means to wash. Lavarse means to wash oneself. Unless you are a baby, you have to wash yourself so use lavarse. Read this chart showing how to conjugate lavarse.

TO WASH ONESELF = LAVARSE (PRESENT TENSE)

I wash myself. = Me lavo.	We wash ourselves. = Nos lavamos.
You wash yourself. (informal, singular) = Te lavas.	You wash yourself. (plural, Spain) = Os laváis.
He washes himself. = Se lava. She washes herself. = Se lava. You wash yourself. (formal, singular) = Se lava.	They wash themselves. = Se lavan. You wash yourself. (formal, plural) = Se lavan.

OTHER REFLEXIVE VERBS:

To go to bed = Acostarse (o-ue)
To shave = Afeitarse
To bathe = Bañarse

To put on makeup = Maquillarse
To wake up = Despertarse (e-ie)
To put on clothes = Ponerse la ropa

PRESENT PROGRESSIVE

Here is how you say that something is in progress -ing

For example; I am trying to learn. = Estoy tratando de aprender.
Use this with an event actually in progress, not future intent.
Here is how you conjugate the present progressive

-AR VERB:

estar + verbstem + ando= I am verb-ing
Estoy trabajando. = I am working

-ER/-IR VERB:

estar + verbstem + iendo
Estoy comiendo. = I am eating.

PRESENT PROGRESSIVE IRREGULARS:

1. -er verbs ending in a,e,o replace i with y
2. -ir stem changing verbs use preterite form
3. some present irregulars like diciendo

EXTRA GRAMMAR: -AR PRESENT TENSE

Basic verb conjugation If you are allergic to grammar, you might want to skip this section all together. If you want a basic crash course in grammar because you are taking a Spanish course or have a child taking Spanish in high school, please continue reading. Understanding the subject pronouns is the key to verb conjugation. Remember that conjugation is matching nouns with the verb. Here are the subject pronouns:

I = yo	we = nosotros
you (informal, singular) = tú	you (plural, Spain) = vosotros
he = él She = ella you (formal, singular) = usted Note: Ud. is the abbreviation for usted.	they (at least one male in the group) = ellos they (all female group) = ellas you (formal, plural) = ustedes Note: Uds. is the abbreviation for ustedes.

In this book, we focus on the more formal communication. Therefore there isn't much reference to the tú or vosotros forms of the verb. Tú is used around close friends and family. Vosotros is used primarily in Spain. In the Americas most speakers substitute the vosotros form with the ustedes. Remember if you are unsure how to conjugate and the noun is singular, chances are it's the él, ella, usted form of the verb. If you are not sure how to conjugate the verb and the noun is plural, go with the ellos, ellas, ustedes form of the verb. A final note on the subject pronouns is nosotros can be used when it says nosotros or if it refers to two people as "we." For example, if the sentence says, "Carlos y yo," then the verb would be conjugated in the nosotros form.

Basic verb conjugation These are the regular present tense endings:

-AR / -ER / -IR PRESENT TENSE:

yo	+ o	nosotros	+ amos / -emos / -imos
tú	+ as / -es / -es	vosotros	+ áis / -éis / -ís
él ella usted	+ a / -e / - e	ellos ellas ustedes	+ an / -en /- en

EXTRA GRAMMAR: PRESENT TENSE VERBS

La Práctica = The Practice: Conjugate the verb in the present tense.

Conjugate the verb to match the subject of each sentence.

1. **ACABAR:**
   Yo _____
   Usted _____
   Nosotros _____
   Ellos _____

2. **APRENDER:**
   Yo _____
   Luis _____
   Nosotros _____
   Franco y María _____

3. **VIVIR:**
   Yo _____
   Susana _____
   Zorro y yo _____
   Laura y Catarina _____

4. **HABLAR:**
   Yo _____ todo el día.
   Mi mamá _____ por teléfono.

5. **HABLAR:**
   Mi hijo, Juanito _____ mucho.
   Mi hija y mi esposo no _____ tanto como yo.

6. **HABLAR:**
   Mi hija, Elena _____ mucha.
   ¿Usted _____ en el trabajo?

7. **LEER:**
   Yo _____ muchos libros.
   ¿Usted _____ mucho?
   Pancho _____ en la sala.

8. **LEER:**
   Las maestros _____ a sus clases.
   En la clase, nosotros _____ juntos.

9. **LEER:**
   Julia _____ a sus hijos cada noche.
   La biblioteca tiene muchos libros para _____.

10. **ASISTIR:**
    Yo _____ a la clase.
    Noe _____ a la clase.
    Lalo y Juana _____ a la fiesta.

11. **ASISTIR:**
    Nosotros _____ a la reunión.
    ¿Cristina, te gusta _____ a sus clases?

EXTRA GRAMMAR: BOOT VERBS

Boot verbs = Stem changing verbs in the present tense:

Not all 10,000 verbs in Spanish follow the basic pattern of the regular verbs –ar, -er, and –ir. The rule breakers must be memorized. Those irregularities are designed to make the verbs flow better when speaking. For example, some verbs are stem changing verbs and other verbs are irregular in the first person only. The purpose of this book is not to teach all the basics of Spanish grammar. Buying a basic grammar book would help with that. However, with a fundamental understanding of the rule breakers, you will be able to eliminate some basic conversational errors and use a dictionary correctly.

For example, if you look up the verb poder in your dictionary, this verb means "to be able or can." Right after the word poder, you might see an abbreviation (v. irr.). This means the word is a verb and irregular in the present tense. The word poder n. mascl. is something different. This tells you poder is also used as a noun. El poder means the power. You should be familiar with all of the abbreviations in your dictionary to insure you are using the word correctly.

Here are a few of the basics of irregular verb conjugation. This isn't intended to be a complete list, but it's intended to jar a few flashbacks to Spanish 101. There are four basic types of stem changing verbs (e-ie, o-ue, e-i, and u-ue). We will conjugate an example of each. Enjoy!

Notice all the verb conjugations except the nosotros and vosotros forms have a spelling change in the stem. Some teachers call these types of verbs boot verbs. If you outline around all the verbs that have a spelling change in the stem, the outline shape will be a boot.

To think = Pensar (ie) present tense irregular:

I think. = Yo pienso.	We think. = Nosotros pensamos.
You think.= Tú piensas. (informal, singular)	You think. (plural, Spain) = Vosotros pensáis.
He thinks.= Él piensa. She thinks.= Ella piensa. You think. = Usted piensa. **(formal, singular)**	They think. = Ellos piensan. **(at least one male in the group)** They think. = Ellas piensan. **(all female group)** You think.= Ustedes piensan. **(formal, plural)**

Use the endings of the regular –ar, -er, and –ir endings. If you forgot, find the –ar/-er-ir endings in the book. The spell change in the stem makes this verb irregular. Here are some other common verbs with the e-ie stem changes.

| to prefer = preferir | to want = querer | to close = cerrar |
| to begin = empezar | to understand = entender | to lose = perder |

EXTRA GRAMMAR: BOOT VERBS

When you practice conjugating verbs, get in the habit of conjugating the singular pronouns on one side and the plural pronouns on the other side. This will help you to see the patterns and memorize the irregular verbs.

TO BE ABLE TO, CAN = PODER (UE) PRESENT TENSE IRREGULAR:

I can. = Yo puedo.	We can. = Nosotros podemos.
You can. = Tú puedes. (informal, singular)	You can. = Vosotros podéis. (plural, Spain)
He can. = Él puede. She can. = Ella puede. You can. = Usted puede. (formal, singular)	They can. = Ellos pueden. (at least one male) They can. = Ellas pueden. (all females) You can. = Ustedes pueden. (formal, plural)

These are six other common verbs with the o-ue stem change:

to count, to tell = contar   to cost = costar   to return = volver
to sleep = dormir   to eat lunch = almorzar   to remember = recordar

TO ASK FOR = PEDIR (IE) PRESENT TENSE IRREGULAR:

I ask for = yo pido	we ask for = nosotros pedimos
you ask for = tú pides (informal, singular)	you ask for = vosotros pedís (plural, Spain)
he asks for = él pide she asks for = ella pide you ask for = usted pide (formal, singular)	they ask for = ellos piden (at least one male) they ask for = ellas piden (all females) you ask for = ustedes piden (formal, plural)

Another common verb with the e-i stem change is to repeat = repetir

EXTRA GRAMMAR: IRREGULAR PRESENT TENSE.

TO PLAY A SPORT = JUGAR (UE) PRESENT TENSE IRREGULAR:

I play. = Yo juego. =.	We play. = Nosotros jugamos.
You play. = Tú juegas. (informal, singular)	You play. = Vosotros jugáis. (plural, Spain)
He plays. = Él juega. She plays. = Ella juega. You play. Usted juega. (formal, singular)	They play. = Ellos juegan. (at least one male) They play. = Ellas juegan. (all females) You play. = Ustedes juegan. (formal, plural)

PRESENT TENSE- FIRST PERSON IRREGULAR VERBS:

There are some verbs in the present tense that are irregular in only the yo form of the verb. These are some of the most common irregular verbs in the present tense:

    to know a fact = saber =.   Yo sé.
    to know a person or place. = conocer   Yo conozco.

The verbs ending in the letters –go are known in some circles as Go-Go verbs. Go-Go verbs are like Go-Go dancers because they both take off items. The dancers shed clothes and the verbs shed the –go ending after the yo form. Now, aren't you glad you are reading the grammar section? For more information see #29 = veintinueve.

    to do, make = hacer   I make. = Yo hago.
    to put = poner   I put. = Yo pongo.
    to bring = traer   I bring. = Yo traigo.
    to leave = salir   I leave. Yo salgo.
    to come = venir   I come. = Yo vengo.
                                       (This is also an e--ie stem changing verb.)
    to have = tener   I have. Yo tengo. (This is an e--ie stem changing verb.)

EXTRA GRAMMAR: REGULAR PRETERITE

Preterite usually corresponds to the English –ed or did. Preterite is used to describe actions and events that happened once in the past as well as events that happened a specified number of times. These are the endings for the regular preterite tense:

To buy = Comprar (-ar preterite):

I bought. = Yo compré.	We bought. = Nosotros compramos.
You bought. (informal, singular) = Tú compraste.	You bought. (plural, Spain) = Vosotros comprasteis.
He bought. = Él compró. She bought. = Ella compró. You bought. (formal, singular) = Usted compró.	They bought. (at least one male) = Ellos compraron. They bought. (all females) = Ellas compraron. You bought. (formal, plural) = Ustedes compraron.

To sell = Vender (-er preterite):

I sold. = Yo vendí.	We sold. = Nosotros vendimos.
You sold. (informal, singular) = Tú vendiste.	You sold. (plural, Spain) = Vosotros vendisteis.
He sold. = Él vendió. She sold. = Ella vendió. You sold. (formal, singular) = Usted vendió.	They sold. = Ellos vendieron. They sold. = Ellas vendieron. You sold. (formal, plural) = Ustedes vendieron.

EXTRA GRAMMAR: MORE PRETERITE.

AL FINAL
87 OCHENTA Y SIETE

To receive = Recibir (-ir preterite):

I received. = Yo recibí.	We received. = Nosotros recibimos.
You received. (informal, singular) = Tú recibiste.	You received. (plural, Spain) = Vosotros recibisteis.
He received. = Él recibió. She received. = Ella recibió. You received. (formal, singular) = Usted recibió.	They received. = Ellos recibieron. They received. = Ellas recibieron. You received. (formal, plural) = Ustedes recibieron.

Verbs ending in the letters –car, gar, and zar have a spelling change only in the yo form.

- buscar: Yo busqué. = I searched for.

- pagar: Yo pagué. = I paid.

- almorzar : Yo almorcé. = I ate lunch.

IRREGULAR PRETERITE

We have covered the basics of regular conjugation in the preterite past tense. However, do all 10,000 verbs have this regular conjugation? It would be wonderful if it did, but we are not that lucky. Some verbs are irregular in the preterite and must be memorized. Fortunately there are a few tricks to make this memorization come a little easier.

Many irregular preterite verbs end like this:

yo	– e	nosotros	- imos
tú	– iste	vosotros	- eis
él ella usted	- o - o - o	ellos ellas ustedes	-ieron -ieron -ieron

EXTRA GRAMMAR: IRREGULAR PRETERITE

AL FINAL — 88 OCHENTA Y OCHO

Here is an example of an irregular preterite:

TO WISH, TO WANT = QUERER (IRREGULAR PRETERITE):

I wanted. = Yo quise.	We wanted. = Nosotros quisimos.
You wanted. (informal, singular) = Tú quisiste.	You wanted. (plural, Spain) = Vosotros quisisteis.
He wanted. = Él quiso. She wanted. = Ella quiso. You wanted. (formal, singular) = Usted quiso.	They wanted. = Ellos quisieron. They wanted. = Ellas quisieron. You wanted. (formal, plural) = Ustedes quisieron.

Notice the preterite stem remains consistent throughout the conjugation and the endings come from the irregular preterite endings.

These are some of the irregular preterite verbs along with their preterite stems. The subject pronouns not listed will be conjugated in the regular form of preterite.:

- andar = to walk (Anduv) Yo anduve. Usted anduvo. Ellos anduvieron.

- caber = to fit into (Cup) Yo cupe. Usted cupo. Ellos cupieron.

- estar = to be (Estuv) Yo estuve. Usted estuvo. Ellos estuvieron.

- poder = to be able, can (Pud) Yo pude. Usted pudo. Ellos pudieron.

- poner = to put (Pus) Yo puse. Usted puso. Ellos pusieron.

- querer = to wish, want (Quis) Yo quise. Usted quiso. Ellos quisieron.

- saber = to know (Sup) Yo supe. Usted supo. Ellos supieron.

- tener = to have (Tuv) Yo tuve. Usted tuvo. Ellos tuvieron.

- venir = to come (Vin) Yo vine. Usted vino. Ellos vinieron.

EXTRA GRAMMAR: IRREGULAR PRETERITE CONTINUED

Here are some of the irregular preterite verbs that you may have to memorize, since they don't exactly follow a pattern. These first four verbs will have a j in the stem and also drop the i in the ellos, ellas, and ustedes form. Here is an example;

TO BRING = TRAER (IRREGULAR PRETERITE):

I brought. = Yo traje.	We brought = Nosotros trajimos.
You brought. (informal, singular) = Tú trajiste.	You brought (plural, Spain) = Vosotros trajisteis.
He brought. = Él trajo. She brought. = Ella trajo. You brought (informal, singular) = Usted trajo.	They brought. = Ellos trajeron. They brought. = Ellas trajeron. You brought. (Fomal, plural) = Ustedes trajeron.

3 more verbs are similiar to traer in the preterite tense:

- to say, to tell = decir(dij) Yo dije. Usted dijo. Ellos dijeron.

- to conduct = conducir (Conduj) Yo conduje. Usted condujo. Ellos condujeron.

- to translate = traducir (Traduj) Yo traduje. Usted tradujo. Ellos tradujeron.

Here is one of the few verbs with two preterite stems (hic and hiz). Here is an example;

TO DO OR TO MAKE = HACER (IRREGULAR PRETERITE):

I did. = Yo hice.	We did. = Nosotros hicimos.
You did. (informal, singular) = Tú hiciste.	You did. (plural, Spain) = Vosotros hicisteis.
He did. = Él hizo. She did. = Ella hizo. You did. (formal, singular) = Usted hizo.	They did. = Ellos hicieron. They did. = Ellas hicieron. You did. (formal, plural) = Ustedes hicieron.

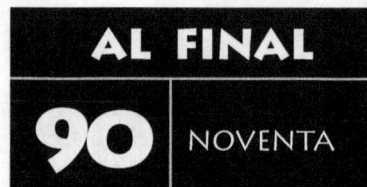

EXTRA GRAMMAR: IRREGULAR PRETERITE

Although they are classified as irregular preterites, the verbs ver = to see and dar = to give are very similar in the preterite. Here is the conjugation for dar; for ver just substitute the d with a v.

TO GIVE = DAR (IRREGULAR PRETERITE):

I gave. = Yo di.	We gave. = Nosotros dimos.
You gave. (informal, singular) = Tú diste.	You gave. (plural, Spain) = Vosotros disteis.
He gave. = Él dio. She gave. = Ella dio. You gave. (formal, singular) = Usted dio.	They gave. = Ellos dieron. They gave. = Ellas dieron. You gave. (formal, plural) = Ustedes dieron.

The final verbs that are irregular in the preterite are the verbs to go=ir and to be = ser. The good news is the conjugations are identical. This table is also found in 151 = ciento cincuenta y uno.

TO BE= SER + TO GO = IR (IRREGULAR PRETERITE):

I was. I went. = Yo fui.	We were. We went. = Nosotros fuimos.
He was. He went. = Él fue.	She was. She went. = Ella fue.
You were. You went. (singular)= Usted fue. They were. They went. = Ellos fueron.	They were. They went. (all female) = Ellas fueron. You were. You went. (plural) = Ustedes fueron.

EXTRA GRAMMAR: SKATEBOARD VERBS

AL FINAL
91 NOVENTA Y UNO

SKATEBOARD VERBS

Skateboard verbs are stem changing -ir verbs that only change in the third person preterite. Here is an example;

TO ASK FOR = PEDIR

I asked for = yo pedí

you asked for = Tú pediste

we asked for = nosotros pedimos

you asked for (plural, Spain) = vosotros pedisteis

> he asked for= él pidió.
> they asked for = ellos pidieron
> she asked for = ella pidió
> they asked for (all female) = ellas pidieron
>
> you asked for (singular)= usted pidió
> you asked for (plural) = ustedes pidieron

E CHANGES TO I

to obtain = conseguir

to have fun = divertirse

to ask for = pedir

to prefer = preferir

to follow = seguir

to feel = sentirse

to serve = servir

to dress yourself = vestirse

to wake yourself up = despedirse

O CHANGES TO U

morir = to die

dormir = to sleep

Note: The yo and ella form do have accent marks.

EXTRA GRAMMAR: IRREGULAR PRETERITE & IMPERFECT

Verbs ending in –er and –ir and have a vowel at the end of the stem require a "y" in the preterite third person form. Here is an example;

TO READ = LEER:

I read. = Yo leí.	We read. = Nosotros leímos.
You read. (informal, singular) = Tú leíste.	You read. (plural, Spain) = Vosotros leísteis.
He reads. = Él leyó. She reads. = Ella leyó.	They read. = Ellos leyeron. They read. = Ellas leyeron.
You read. (formal, singular) = Usted leyó.	They read. (formal, plural) = Ustedes leyeron.

A few other examples are:

to hear = oir

to fall = caer

IMPERFECT PAST TENSE

Imperfect is used to talk about events or conditions in progress at a particular point in the past, often while something else was happening. In English this is translated as: was/were….ing. The imperfect past tense is used in these four situations:

1. To describe conditions ongoing in the past. For example, physical characteristics, states of mind, weather, and emotions, as well as age.
2. To talk about events ongoing (in progress) in the past. Including simultaneous events expressed with mientras. Also look for the word cuando. The ongoing action will be in imperfect and the interrupting action will be in preterite.
3. The ir + a is almost always in the imperfect.
4. The imperfect is used to tell time in the past and talk about habitual events. Look for the Spanish words, siempre or generalmente or todos los días.

EXTRA GRAMMAR: IRREGULAR IMPERFECT

In the imperfect past tense there are no stem or spelling changes. The yo and ella forms are the same. This chart shows how to conjugate regular imperfect verbs:

-AR IMPERFECT PAST TENSE:

yo	– aba	nosotros	- ábamos
tú	- abas	vosotros	- abais
él	- aba	ellos	- aban
ella	- aba	ellas	- aban
usted	- aba	ustedes	- aban

-ER AND -IR IMPERFECT PAST TENSE:

yo	– ía	nosotros	- íamos
tú	- ías	vosotros	- íais
él	- ía	ellos	- ían
ella	- ía	ellas	- ían
usted	- ía	ustedes	- ían

THERE ARE ONLY THREE IRREGULAR IMPERFECT PAST TENSE VERBS:

to be = ser: Yo era. Tú eras. Alicia era. Nosotros èramos. Vosotros erais. Ellos eran.

to go = ir: Yo iba. Tú ibas. Timoteo iba. Nosotros íbamos. Vosotros ibais. Ellos iban.

to see = ver: Yo veía. Tú veías. Jaime veía. Nosotros veíamos. Vosotros veíais. Ellos veían.

EXTRA GRAMMAR: PRETERITE VS. IMPERFECT

PRETERITE VERSUS IMPERFECT

La Práctica = The Practice: Conjugate the verb in either the preterite or imperfect past depending on which is appropriate.

1. La clase de español _____ (ser) muy divertida en nuestra compañía.

2. Nosotros _____ (aprender) mucho.

3. En la primera clase, yo _____ (estudiar) frases importantes.

4. También en esta clase yo _____ (usar) un CD de frases.

5. ¿Usted _____ (escuchar) el CD?

6. María, Indira, Paca, y Cristina _____ (practicar) mucho.

7. Teresa y Angelica _____ (hacer) comida buena.

8. Gracias a Miguel, él _____ (arreglar) las sillas cada semana.

9. Jorge y Juana _____ (grabar) una película.

10. Mónica _____ (hablar) por teléfono en español con los clientes.

11. La maestra Julia _____ (estar) triste por decir, "¡Adiós!"

Note: All grammar answers are in the Answer Key

Don't worry if you struggled with this exercise. This takes some practice. Even if you use the wrong past tense, you will probably be understood and forgiven by the native speakers. With practice you will get better at this conjugation and the answers will start to sound right. Please keep this information handy. If you ever decide to take another Spanish class, you will find the information in this extra grammar section very useful. There are many great Spanish books containing more grammar exercises. If you would like more information and resources, check our Web site, SpanishChatCompany.com

ENGLISH = SPANISH

AL FINAL 95 NOVENTA Y CINCO

a, an = **un, una**	appointment = **cita**	begin, to = **empezar**
about, above = **sobre**	around = **alrededor**	behind = **tras**
absence = **ausencia**	arrive, to = **llegar**	below = **bajo**
achieve = **lograr**	art = **arte**	bench = **banco**
actions = **aciones**	artist = **artista**	best wishes = **felicidades**
address = **dirección**	as = **como**	better = **mejor**
Africa = **África**	assistant = **asistente**	between = **entonces**
after = **después de**	at = **a/en**	big = **grande**
afternoon = **tarde**	aunts = **tías**	biological = **biológico**
agent = **agente**	back = **atrás**	bird = **pájaro**
agency = **agencia**	bad = **mal / mala(o)**	birthday = **cumpleaños**
airplane = **avión**	bank = **banco**	black = **negra(o)**
all = **todo**	basketball = **baloncesto**	blond = **rubia(o)**
almost = **casi**	bathroom = **baño**	blue = **azul**
alone = **solo**	be (changing), to = **estar**	boat = **barco**
already = **ya**	be (permanent), to = **ser**	book = **libro**
also = **también**	be able to = **poder**	border = **frontera**
always = **siempre**	beach = **playa**	bored = **aburrida(o)**
and = **y**	beak = **pico**	boss = **jefe**
animals = **animales**	beautiful = **bonita(o)**	boy = **niño**
anthropology = **antropología**	because of = **por**	bread = **pan**
apartment = **apartamento**	because = **porque**	break, a rest = **descanso**
apple = **manzana**	before = **antes**	breakfast = **desayuno**

AL FINAL — ENGLISH = SPANISH

- bring, to = **traer**
- broccoli = **brócoli**
- brother = **hermano**
- brother-in-law = **cuñado**
- brunette = **morena(o)**
- bull = **toro**
- busy = **ocupada(o)**
- building = **edificio**
- but = **pero**
- butterfly = **mariposa**
- by = **por**
- cake = **pastel**
- call (be named), to = **llamar(se)**
- can, be able to = **poder**
- candy = **dulce**
- car = **carro**
- card = **tarjeta**
- carrot = **zanahoria**
- carry, to = **llevar**
- cashier = **cajero**
- cat = **gata(o)**
- celebrate, to = **celebrar**
- cemetery = **cementerio**

- center = **centro**
- Central America = **América Central**
- certain = **cierto**
- change, to = **cambiar**
- channel = **canal**
- chat, to = **charlar**
- cheese = **queso**
- chicken = **pollo**
- chores = **quehaceres**
- Christmas = **Navidad**
- citizen = **ciudadana(o)**
- city = **ciudad**
- class = **clase**
- clean, to = **limpiar**
- clear = **claro**
- climate = **clima**
- climb, to = **subir**
- clock = **reloj**
- close = **cerca de**
- clothing = **ropa**
- cloudy = **nublado**
- coffee = **café**
- cold = **fría(o)**

- colors = **colores**
- come, to = **venir**
- companion = **compañera(o)**
- company = **compañía**
- cookie = **galleta**
- correct = **correcto**
- cotton = **algodón**
- counselor = **consejera(o)**
- country = **país**
- countryside = **campo**
- cousins = **primos**
- creativity = **creatividad**
- culture = **cultura**
- cup, mug = **taza**
- custom, tradition = **costumbre**
- cute = **bonita(o)**
- dad = **papá**
- dancers = **bailarines**
- dance, to = **bailar**
- danger = **peligro**
- date = **cita** (appointment), **fecha** (calendar)
- daughter = **hija**

ENGLISH = SPANISH

daughter-in-law = **nuera**

day = **día**

dead things = **muertos**

delicious = **rica(o)**

dentist = **dentista**

desk = **escritorio**

dessert = **postre**

dice = **dados**

difficult = **difícil**

direction = **dirección**

director = **director(a)**

diversity = **diversidad**

doctor = **doctor(a)**

dog = **perro**

doll = **muñeca**

dollars = **dólares**

done = **hecho**

do, to = **hacer**

dress = **vestido**

dress, to = **vestir(se)**

drinks = **bebidas**

during = **durante**

each = **cada**

early = **temprano**

earn, to = **ganar**

east = **este / oriente**

Easter = **Pascua**

eat, to = **comer**

eggs, scrambled = **huevos revueltos**

elephant = **elefante**

emotional = **emocionada(o)**

end, to finish = **terminar**

English = **inglés**

enough = **bastante**

evaluation = **evaluación**

everything = **todo**

exam = **examen**

exercise = **ejercicio**

except = **excepto**

excited = **emocionada(o)**

expert = **experta(o)**

fact = **hecho**

fall / fall down, to = **caer(se)**

false = **falso**

family = **familia**

famous = **famosa(o)**

far = **lejos**

fast = **rápido**

father-in-law = **suegro**

father = **padre**

favorite = **favorita(o)**

feel (emotions), to = **sentir(se)**

final project = **proyecto final**

find, to = **encontrar**

finish, to end = **terminar**

fine = **bien**

fire = **fuego**

first = **primero**

fish = **pez**

flag = **bandera**

flowers = **flores**

food = **comida**

football = **fútbol americano**

foreigner = **extranjera(o)**

forest = **bosque**

for = **para / por**

AL FINAL — ENGLISH = SPANISH

fried = **frita(o)**

friend = **amiga(o)**

from = **de / del**

from = **desde**

from time to time = **de vez en cuando**

front = **frente**

fruit = **fruta**

full = **llena(o)**

fun = **divertido**

function, to = **funcionar**

game = **juego / partido** (sport)

garden = **jardín**

generally = **generalmente**

German = **alemán**

gift = **regalo**

girl = **niña**

go (oneself), to = **ir (se)**

go to, to = **ir a**

go up = **subir**

goal = **meta, gol** (sport)

goalie = **portero**

good = **bueno**

goodbye = **adiós**

gorilla = **gorila**

grade = **grado**

grammar = **gramática**

grandparents = **abuelos**

grapes = **uvas**

grill = **parilla / asador**

guide = **guía**

hallway = **pasillo**

ham = **jamón**

hamburger = **hamburguesa**

happily = **felizmente**

have, to = **tener**

health(y) = **salud(able)**

he = **él**

hear = **oír**

heat = **calor**

hello = **hola**

Help! = **¡Socorro!**

help, to = **ayudar**

here = **aquí / acá**

her = **su**

hers = **suya(o)/s**

high = **alto**

highway = **carretera**

him = **lo**

his = **su / suya(o)/s**

history = **historia**

holidays = **días festivos**

homework = **tarea**

horse = **caballo**

hotels = **hoteles**

hour = **hora**

house = **casa**

how = **cómo**

how many = **cuánto**

how much = = **cuánto**

how = **qué**

humidity = **humedad**

hunger = **hambre**

hurry = **prisa**

husband = **esposo**

ice cream = **helado**

if = **si**

important = **importante**

in = **en**

ENGLISH = SPANISH

AL FINAL
99 NOVENTA Y NUEVE

in order to = **para**

independence = **independencia**

inside = **adentro**

instruments = **instrumentos**

interpreter = **interpréte**

interview = **entrevista**

invitation = **invitación**

invited guest = **invitada(o)**

island = **isla**

it = **la / lo**

its = = **su**

I = **yo**

job = **trabajo**

jump, to = **saltar / brincar**

kids = **chica(o)**

kings, magi = **reyes magos**

kitchen = **cocina**

know information, to = **saber**

know someone, someplace, to = **conocer**

lake = **lago**

language = **idioma**

last = **última(o)**

last name = **apellido**

last night = **anoche**

lasted = **duro**

later = **luego**

late = **tarde**

Latin American = **Latinoamericana(o)**

learn, to = **aprender**

left = **izquierda**

legends = **leyendas**

less = **menos**

life = **vida**

like, to = **gustar**

listen = **escuchar**

little = **poco**

live, to = **vivir**

look for, to = **buscar**

look, to = **mirar**

lottery = **lotería**

luck = **suerte**

luggage = **equipaje**

lunch = **almuerzo**

mad = **enojada(o)**

make, to = **hacer**

mammal = **mamífero**

man = **hombre**

manager = **gerente**

manger = **pesebre**

manner = **manera**

many = **muchas(os)**

map = **mapa**

marvelous = **maravilloso**

match (sports) = **partido**

math = **matemáticas**

mayor = **alcalde**

meanwhile = **mientras**

meat = **carne**

meeting = **reunión**

meet, to = **encontrar**

member = **miembra(o)**

menu = **menú**

middle = **mitad**

million = **millón**

milk = **leche**

mine = **mía(o)/s**

AL FINAL
100 CIEN
ENGLISH = SPANISH

minus = **menos**

minute = **minuto**

modern = **moderno**

moment = **momento**

mom = **mamá**

money = **dinero**

monkey = **mono**

month = **mes**

moon = **luna**

more = **más**

morning = **mañana**

mother-in-law = **suegra**

mother = **madre**

movie = **película**

movie theater = **cine**

much = **mucho**

mug = **taza**

museum = **museo**

my = **mi/mis**

myself = **me**

nap = **siesta**

national = **nacional**

near = **cerca**

need, to = **necesitar**

neighbor = **vecina(o)**

neither = **tampoco**

nephew = **sobrino**

never = **nunca**

new = **nueva(o)**

news = **noticias**

next = **próximo**

nice = **simpática(o)**

niece = **sobrina**

night = **noche**

none / no = **ningún**

no = **no**

no one = **nadie**

nor = **ni**

normally = **normalmente**

north = **norte**

not one = **ninguna(o)**

note = **nota**

nothing = **nada**

now = **ahora**

number = **número**

nurse = **enfermera(o)**

of = **de / del**

of course = **claro que sí**

offerings (altars) = **ofrendas**

office = **oficina**

often = **a menudo**

old = **vieja(o)**

older = **mayor**

on = **a / en / sobre**

on top of = **encima**

only = **sólo**

or = **o**

orange (color) = **anaranjada(o)**

orange (fruit) = **naranja**

other = **otra(o)**

our/ours = **nuestra(o)**

outside = **afuera**

over there = **allá**

page = **página**

pair = **pareja**

palace = **palacio**

parade = **desfile**

park = **parque**

ENGLISH = SPANISH

AL FINAL
101 CIENTO Y UNO

part = **parte**	player = **jugador(a)**	quarter (1/4) = **cuarto**
party = **fiesta**	plaza = **plaza**	question = **pregunta**
passenger = **pasajera**	please = **por favor**	quickly = **rápido**
pass, to = **pasar**	pleasure = **gusto**	race (ethnicity) = **raza**
past = **pasada(o)**	plus = **más**	rain, to = **llover**
path = **camino**	pole = **palo**	rainy = **lluvioso**
patience = **paciencia**	poor = **pobre**	ray = **raya**
pay, to = **pagar**	porter = **portero**	ready = **lista(o)**
peace = **paz**	possible = **posible**	receive, to = **recibir**
peak (mountain) = **pico**	possibly = **posiblemente**	recipe = **receta**
pedestrians = **peatones**	poster = **cartel**	red = **roja(o)**
people = **gente**	potato = **papa**	remember, to = **recordar**
perfectly = **perfectamente**	presentation = **presentacíon**	repeat, to = **repetir**
person = **persona**	priest = **sacerdote**	respect = **respeto**
pet = **mascota**	principal = **director(a)**	restaurant = **restaurante**
phrase = **frase**	problem = **problema**	rest = **descanso**
photo = **la foto**	professor = **profesor(a)**	reunion = **reunión**
piece = **pedazo**	program = **programa**	ribbons = **cintas**
place = **lugar**	project, final = **proyecto final**	rice = **arroz**
placemat = **mantel individual**	put (on), to = **poner(se)**	rich = **rica(o)**
plant = **planta**	pyramids = **pirámides**	right = **derecha**
play, to = **jugar**	quality = **calidad**	river = **río**
		room = **cuarto**

AL FINAL — ENGLISH = SPANISH

row = **fila, raya**

run, to = **correr**

saint = **santa**

salad = **ensalada**

say, to = **decir**

school = **escuela**

scholarship, grant = **beca**

scissors = **tijeras**

season = **estación**

see, to = **ver**

sense = **sentido**

server = **mesera(o)**

she = **ella**

shoe = **zapato**

short = **bajo**

shout = **grito**

siblings = **hermanos**

sign, to = **firmar**

sign / poster = **cartel**

since = = **desde**

singer = **cantante**

single = **solo**

sister = **hermana**

sister-in-law = **cuñada**

slow = **despacia(o) / lenta(o)**

small = **pequeña(o)**

smart = **lista(o)**

smooth = **suave**

snow, to = **nevar**

so = **así**

so many, so much = **tanto**

soccer = **fútbol**

some = **un(os) / una(s) / algunas(os) / algún**

somebody = **alguien**

someone = **alguien**

someone = **alguna(o)**

something = **algo**

sometimes = **a veces**

son = **hijo**

son-in-law = **yerno**

soon = **pronto**

so = **tan**

soul = **alma**

south = **sur**

South America = **América del Sur**

Spain = **España**

Spaniards = **Españoles**

Spanish = **español**

speak, to = **hablar**

special = **especial**

species = **especies**

sport = **deporte**

stairs = **escaleras**

start, to = **empezar**

station = **estación**

statue = **estatua**

stick = **palo**

still = **todavía**

stone = **piedra**

storm = **tormenta**

straight = **derecho**

strawberry = **fresa**

street = **calle**

stripe = **raya**

strong = **fuerte**

student = **estudiante**

ENGLISH = SPANISH

AL FINAL
103 CIENTO Y TRES

study, to = **estudiar**	the = **la / el / las / los**	to her = **le**
such = **tal**	theater = **teatro**	to him = **le**
suitcase = **maleta**	their = **sus**	to me = **me**
summer = **verano**	them (female) = **las**	to them = **les**
sun = **sol**	them = **los**	to you = **le / les**
supermarket = **supermercado**	then = **entonces**	too much = **demasiada(o)**
supper = **cena**	there = **allí**	today = **hoy**
sweets = **dulces**	there is / there are = **hay**	together = **juntos**
system = **sistema**	these = **esos / estas**	tomato = **tomate**
take, to = **llevar / tomar**	they = **ellas(os)**	tomorrow = **mañana**
talk, to = = **hablar**	thirst = **sed**	tourist = **turista**
tall = **alto**	this one = **esta / este**	towards = **hacia**
tea = **té / mate**	those = **esas / estos**	train = **tren**
teacher = **maestra(o)**	those over there = **aquellas(os)**	travel = **viajar**
telephone = **teléfono**	true = **cierto / verdad**	trees = **arboles**
television = **televisión**	throat = **garganta**	trip = **viaje**
tell, to = **decir**	throw, to = **tirar**	try, to = **intentar**
tennis = **tenis**	time = **tiempo / vez**	turkey = **pavo**
thank you = **gracias**	tip = **propina**	uncles = **tíos**
that = **que / tal**	tired = **cansada(o)**	under = **bajo**
that one = **esa / ese**	title = **título**	understand, to **entender**
that one over there = **aquella / aquel**	to = **a**	underwear = **ropa interior**
		unity = **unidad**

AL FINAL

ENGLISH = SPANISH

university = **universidad**

until = **hasta**

U.S.A. = **Estados Unidos de América**

useful = **útil**

usually = **usualmente**

vacation = **vacaciones**

vegetables = **verduras**

very = **muy**

visit, to = **visitar**

voices = **voces**

volcanos = **volcanes**

voluntad = **willpower**

wait, to = **esperer**

wake up, to = **despertar**

want, to = **querer**

watch = **reloj**

watch, to = **mirar**

water (with no bubbles) = **agua sin gas**

water, sparkling = **agua con gas**

waterfall = **catarata**

watermelon = **sandía**

way = **manera**

wear, to = **llevar**

weather = **tiempo / clima**

weekend = **fin de semana**

week = **semana**

weigh, to = **pesar**

welcome = **bienvenida(o)/s**

well = **bien**

we = **nosotros**

west = **oeste**

what = **qué**

when = **cuándo**

where = **dónde**

which = **cuál**

whichever = **cualquier**

which = **qué**

white = **blanca(o)**

Who? = **quién**

why = **por qué**

wife = **esposa**

win = **ganar**

with = **con**

without = **sin**

woman (women) = **mujer(es)**

wood = **madera**

work = **trabajo**

work, to = **trabajar**

workers = **trabajadores**

works of art = **obras de arte**

world = **mundo**

worse = **peor**

wrist = **muñeca**

write, to = **escribir**

year = **año**

yellow = **amarilla(o)**

yes = **sí**

yesterday = **ayer**

yogurt = **yogur**

you all (formal) = **ustedes**

you (formal) = **usted**

younger = **menor**

youngster = **chica(o)**

you're welcome = **de nada**

yourself/yourselves = **se**

your = **sus**

yours = **suya(o)/s**

ESPAÑOL = INGLÉS

AL FINAL

105 CIENTO Y CINCO

- **a** = to / at / on
- **a menudo** = often
- **a veces** = sometimes
- **abuelos** = grandparents
- **aburrida(o)** = bored
- **acá** = here
- **adentro** = inside
- **adiós** = goodbye
- **afuera** = outside
- **agencia** = agency
- **agente** = agent
- **agua sin gas** = water-no gas
- **agua con gas** = sparkling water
- **ahora** = now
- **alcade** = mayor
- **alemán** = German
- **algo** = something
- **algodón** = cotton
- **alguien** = someone / somebody
- **algún** = some
- **alguna(o)** = some, someone
- **allá** = over there
- **allí** = there
- **alma** = soul
- **almuerzo** = lunch
- **alrededor** = around
- **alto** = tall, high
- **amarilla(o)** = yellow
- **América Central** = Central America
- **América del Sur** = South America
- **amigos** = friends
- **anaranjada(o)** = orange
- **animales** = animals
- **año** = year
- **anoche** = last night
- **antes** = before
- **antropología** = anthropology
- **apartamento** = apartment
- **apellido** = last name
- **aquella / aquel** = that one over there
- **aquellas(os)** = those over there
- **aquí** = here
- **árboles** = trees
- **arroz** = rice
- **arte** = art
- **artista** = artist
- **así** = so
- **asistente** = assistant
- **atrás** = back
- **ausencia** = absence
- **autobus** = bus
- **avenida** = avenue
- **avión** = airplane
- **ayer** = yesterday
- **ayudar** = to help
- **azul** = blue
- **bailar** = to dance
- **bailarines** = dancers
- **bajo** = under / below / short
- **baloncesto** = basketball
- **banco** = bank, bench
- **banderas** = flags
- **baño** = bathroom
- **bastante** = enough
- **bebidas** = drinks

AL FINAL — ESPAÑOL = INGLÉS

beca = scholarship

bien = well, fine

bienvenida(o)/s = welcome

biológico = biological

blanca(o) = white

bonita(o) = beautiful / cute

bosque = forest

brócoli = broccoli

buen(o) = good

buscar = to look for

caballo = horse

cada = each

caer(se) = to fall / fall down

café = coffee / brown / cafe

cajero = cashier

calor = heat

calidad = quality

calle = street

cambiar = to change

camino = path, way

campo = countryside

canal = channel

cansada(o) = tired

cantante = singer

carne = meat

carretera = highway

carros = cars

cartel = poster / sign

casa = house

casi = almost

catarata = waterfall

celebrar = to celebrate

cementario = cemetery

cena = supper / dinner

centro = center

cerca de = near

charlar = to chat

chica(o) = youngster / kid

cierto = true, certain

cine = movie theater

cintas = ribbons

cita = appointment / date

ciudad = city

ciudadana(o) = citizen

claro = clear, of course

clase = class

clima = climate, weather

cocina = kitchen

cocodrilo = crocodile

colores = colors

comer = to eat

comida = food

como = as

cómo = how?

compañera(o) = colleague

compañía = company

con = with

concurso = contest

conocer = to know someone/ someplace

consejera(o) = counselor

correcta/o = correct

costumbre = customs / tradition

creatividad = creativity

cuál = which?

cualquier = whichever

cuándo = when

cuánto = how many/ how much

ESPAÑOL = INGLÉS

AL FINAL — 107 CIENTO Y SIETE

cuarto = room, quarter

cuento = story

cultura = culture

cumpleaños = birthday

cuñada = sister-in-law

cuñado = brother-in-law

dados = dice

dar = to give

de / del = of / from

de nada = you're welcome

de vez en cuando = from time to time

decir = to say / tell

demasiada(o) = too much

dentista = dentist

deportes = sports

derecha = right

derecho = straight

desayuno = breakfast

descanso = rest / break

desde = from / since

desfile = parade

despacio = slow

despertar = to wake up

después de = after

día = day

días festivos = holidays

difícil = difficult

dinero = money

dirección = address / direction

director(a) = director / principal

diversidad = diversity

divertido = fun

doctor(a) = doctor

dólares = dollars

dónde = where

dueña(o) = owner

dulces = candies / sweets

durante = during

duro = last / durable

edificio = building

ejercicio = exercise

él = he

el = the

elefante = elephant

ella = she

ellas(os) = they

emocionada(o) = emotional / excited

empezar = to begin / start

en = in / on / at

encima = on top of

encontrar = to find / meet

enfermera(o) = nurse

enojada(o) = mad

ensalada = salad

entender = to understand

entonces = then

entre = between

entrevista = interview

equipaje = luggage

esa = that one

esas = those

escaleras = stairs / ladder

escribir = to write

escritorio = desk

escuchar = to listen

escuela = school

AL FINAL

ESPAÑOL = INGLÉS

esas = those

ese = that one

esos = these

España = Spain

español = Spanish

Españoles = Spaniards

especial = special

especies = species

esperer = to wait

esposa = wife

esposo = husband

esta = this one

estación = station / season

Estados Unidos de América = U.S.A.

estar = to be (changing)

estas = these

estatua = statue

este = this one / East

estos = those

estudiante = student

estudiar = to study

evaluación = evaluation

examen = exam

excepto = except

experta(o) = expert

extranjera(o) = foreigner

falso = false

familia = family

famosa(o) = famous

favorita(o) = favorite

fecha = date (on calendar)

felicidades = best wishes

felicitaciones = congratulations

felizmente = happily

fiesta = party

fin de semana = weekend

firmar = to sign

flores = flowers

foto = photo (la)

frase = phrase

frecuencia = frecuency

frente = front

fresa = strawberry

frío = cold

frita(o) = fried

frontera = border

fruta = fruit

fuego = fire

fuerte = strong

funcionar = to function

fútbol = soccer

fútbol americano = football

galleta = cookie

ganar = to earn / win

garganta = throat

gata(o) = cat

generalmente = generally

gente = people

gerente = manager

gorilla = gorila

gracias = thank you

grado = grade

gramática = grammar

grande = big

grito = shout

guía = guide

gustar = to like

hablar = to talk / speak

hacer = to do / make

ESPAÑOL = INGLÉS

AL FINAL
109 CIENTO Y NUEVE

hacia = towards

hambre = hunger

hamburguesa = hamburger

hasta = until

hay = there is / there are

hecho = fact / done

helado = ice cream

hermana = sister

hermano = brother

hermanos = siblings

hija = daughter

hijo = son

historia = history

hola = hello

hombre = man

hora = hour

hoteles = hotels

hoy = today

huevos (revueltos) = (scrambled) eggs

humedad = humidity

idioma = language

iglesia = church

importante = important

independencia = independence

inglés = English

instrumentos = instruments

intentar = to try

interpréte = interpreter

invitación = invitation

invitada(o) = invited guest

ir(se) / ir a = to go (oneself) / to go to

isla = island

izquierda = left

jamón = ham

jardín = garden

jefe = boss

juego = game

jugador = player

jugar = to play

juntos = together

la = the / you / her / it

lago = lake

las = the / you / them (female)

le = to you / to her / to him

leche = milk

leer = to read

lejos = far

les = to you / to them

leyendas = legends

libro = book

limpiar = to clean

listo = ready / smart

llamar(se) = to call (be named)

llegar = to arrive

llena(o) = full

llevar = to carry / wear / take away

llover = to rain

lluvioso = rainy

lo = it / him

lograr = acheive

los = the / you / them

lotería = lottery

luego = later

lugar = place

luna = moon

AL FINAL

ESPAÑOL = INGLÉS

madera = wood

madre = mother

maestra(o) = teacher

mal(a)(o) = bad

maletas = suitcases

mamá = mom

mammal = mamífero

mañana = tomorrow / morning

manera = way / manner

manzana = apple

mapa = map

maravilloso = marvelous

mariposa = butterfly

más = more / plus

mascota = pet

mate = South American tea

matemáticas = math

mayor(es) = older

me = myself / me / to me

mediante = by means of

mejor = better

menor(es) = younger

menos = less / minus

menú = menu

mes = month

mesera(o) = server

meta = goal

mi/mis = my

mía(o)/s = mine

miembra(o) = member

mientras = meanwhile

millón = million

minuto = minute

mirar = to look, watch

mitad = middle

moderna(o) = modern

momento = moment

mono = monkey

morena(o) = brunette

muchas(os) = many

mucho = much

muertos = dead things

mujer(es) = woman (women)

mundo = world

muñeca(o) = doll, wrist

museo = museum

muy = very

nacional = national

nada = nothing

nadie = no one

naranja = orange

Navidad = Christmas

necesitar = to need

negra(o) = black

ni = nor

nevar = to snow

niña(o) = girl (boy)

ningún = no, none

ninguna(o) = not one

no = no

noche = night

normalmente = normally

norte = north

nosotros = we

nota = note

noticias = news

nublado = cloudy

nuera = daughter-in-law

nuestra(o) = our / ours

ESPAÑOL = INGLÉS

AL FINAL
111 CIENTO ONCE

nueva(o) = new	**parque** = park	**pesebre** = manger
número = number	**parrilla** = grill	**pez** = fish
nunca = never	**parte** = part	**pico** = peak (mountain) / beak
o = or	**partido** = game / sport match	**piedra** = stone
obras de arte = works of art	**pasada(o)** = past	**pirámides** = pyramids
ocupada(o) = busy	**pasajera** = passenger	**piso** = floor
oeste = west	**pasar** = to pass	**planta** = plant
oficina = office	**Pascua** = Easter	**playa** = beach
ofrendas = offerings (altars)	**pasillo** = hallway	**pobre** = poor
oír = to hear	**pasteles** = cakes	**poco** = little
otra(o) = other	**pavo** = turkey	**poder** = can / to be able to
paciencia = patience	**paz** = peace	**pollo** = chicken
padre = father	**peatones** = pedestrians	**poner(se)** = to put (on)
país = country	**pedazo** = piece	**por** = for / by / because of
pagina = page	**película** = movie	**por favor** = please
pájaro = bird	**peligro(so)** = danger(ous)	**por qué** = why
palo = pole, stick	**peor** = worse	**porque** = because
pan = bread	**pequeña(o)** = small	**portero** = goalie / porter
papá = dad	**perfectamente** = perfectly	**posible** = possible
papa = potato	**pero** = but	**posiblemente** = possibly
para = for/in order to	**perro** = dog	**postre** = dessert
pareja = pair	**persona** = person	**pregunta** = question
parientes = relatives	**pesar** = to weigh	**presentación** = presentation

AL FINAL — ESPAÑOL = INGLÉS

- **primero** = first
- **primos** = cousins
- **prisa** = hurry
- **problema** = problem
- **programa** = program
- **profesor(a)** = professor
- **pronto** = soon
- **propina** = tip
- **próximo** = next
- **proyecto** = project
- **qué** = what / which / how
- **que** = that
- **quehacers** = chores
- **querer** = to want
- **queso** = cheese
- **quién** = Who?
- **rápido** = quickly / fast
- **raya** = row, ray, stripe
- **raza** = race (ethnicity)
- **receta** = recipe
- **recibir** = to receive
- **recordar** = to remember
- **regalos** = gifts
- **reloj** = clock, watch
- **repetir** = to repeat
- **respeto** = respect
- **restaurante** = restaurant
- **reunión** = meeting / reunion
- **reyes magos** = kings (magi)
- **rica(o)** = rich / delicious
- **río** = river
- **roja(o)** = red
- **ropa** = clothing
- **ropa interior** = underwear
- **rubia(o)** = blond
- **saber** = to know information
- **sacerdote** = priest
- **salir** = to leave / go out
- **saltar** = to jump
- **salud(able)** = health(y)
- **sandía** = watermelon
- **santa** = saint
- **se** = yourself / yourselves
- **sed** = thirst
- **semana** = week
- **sentido** = sense
- **sentir(se)** = to feel (emotions)
- **ser** = to be (permanent)
- **si** = if
- **sí** = yes
- **siempre** = always
- **siesta** = nap
- **simpática(o)** = nice
- **sin** = without
- **sistema** = system
- **sobre** = on / above / about
- **sobrina** = niece
- **sobrino** = nephew
- **¡Socorro!** = Help!
- **sol** = sun
- **solo** = alone / single / only
- **su / sus** = your / her / his / its / their
- **subir** = to climb / go up / board
- **suave** = smooth
- **suegra** = mother-in-law
- **suegro** = father-in-law
- **suerte** = luck
- **supermercado** = supermarket

ESPAÑOL = INGLÉS

AL FINAL — **113** CIENTO TRECE

sur = south

suya(o)/s = yours / hers / his

tal = that / such

también = also

tampoco = neither / also do not

tanto = so many / so much

tarde = late/afternoon

tarea = homework

tarjeta = card

taza = mug, cup

teatro = theater

teléfono = telephone

televisión = television

temprano = early

tener = to have

tenis = tennis

terminar = to finish / end

tiempo = time / weather

tijeras = scissors

tíos = aunts and uncles

tirar = to throw

título = title

todavía = still

todo = all / everything

tomar = to take

tomate = tomato

tormenta = storm

toro = bull

trabajadores = workers

trabajar = to work

trabajo = work/job

traer = to bring

tras = behind / after

tren = train

turista = tourist

última(o) = last

un / una(o)/s = a, an, some

unidad = unity

universidad = university

usted = you (formal)

ustedes = you all (formal)

usualmente = usually

útil = useful

uva = grape

vacaciones = vacation

vecina(o) = neighbor

venir = to come

ver = to see

verano = summer

verdura = vegetable

vestido = dress / outfit

vestir(se) = to dress

vez(veces) = time(s)

viajar = travel

viaje = trip

vida = life

vieja(o) = old

viento = wind

visitar = to visit

vivir = to live

volcanes = volcanos

voluntad = willpower

y = and

ya = already

yerno = son-in-law

yo = I

yogur = yogurt

zanahoria = carrot

zapato = shoe

VERB TABLE 114

	YO = I	ELLA / ÉL / USTED = SHE / HE / YOU	NOSOTROS = WE	YOU PLURAL / THEY = USTEDES / ELLOS
ARRIVE / REACH = LLEGAR*				
PRESENT	llego I arrive / reach	llega one arrives / reaches	llegamos we arrive / reach	llegan two or more arrive / reach
PRETERITE PAST	llegué I arrived / reached	llegó one subject arrived / reached	llegamos we arrived / reached	llegaron two or more subjects arrived / reached
IMPERFECT PAST	llegaba I arrived / reached	llegaba one subject arrived / reached	llegábamos we arrived / reached	llegaban two or more subjects arrived / reached
ASK FOR / ORDER = PEDIR*				
PRESENT	pido I ask for / order	pide one asks for / orders	pedimos we ask for / order	piden two or more ask for / order
PRETERITE PAST	pedí I asked for / ordered	pidió one asked for / ordered	pedimos we asked for / ordered	pidieron two or more asked for / ordered
IMPERFECT PAST	pedía I asked for / ordered	pedía one asked for / ordered	pedíamos we asked for / ordered	pedían two or more asked for / ordered
ATTEND / ASSIST / BE PRESENT = ASISTIR				
PRESENT	asisto I attend / assist / am present	asiste one subject attends / assists / is present	asistimos we attend / assist / are present	asisten two or more subjects attend / assist / are present
PRETERITE PAST	asistí I attended / assisted / presented	asistió one subject attended / assisted / presented	asistimos we attended / assisted / presented	asistieron two or more subjects attended / assisted / presented
IMPERFECT PAST	asistía I attended / assisted / presented	asistía one subject attended / assisted / presented	asistíamos we attended / assisted / presented	asistían two or more subjects attended / assisted / presented
BE - CHANGING = ESTAR*				
PRESENT	estoy I am	está one subject is	estamos we are	están two or more subjects are
PRETERITE PAST	estuve I was	estuvo one subject was	estuvimos we were	estuvieron two or more subjects were
IMPERFECT PAST	estaba I was	estaba one subject was	estábamos we were	estaban two or more subjects were
BE - PERMANENT = SER*				
PRESENT	soy I am	es one subject is	somos we are	son two or more subjects are
PRETERITE PAST	fui I was	fue one subject was	fuimos we were	fueron two or more subjects were
IMPERFECT PAST	era I was	era one subject was	éramos we were	eran two or more subjects were

* an irregular verb

VERB TABLE 115

	YO = I	ELLA / ÉL / USTED = SHE / HE / YOU	NOSOTROS = WE	YOU PLURAL / THEY = USTEDES / ELLOS
BEGIN = EMPEZAR*				
PRESENT	empiezo I begin	empieza one subject begins	empezamos we begin	empiezan two or more subjects begin
PRETERITE PAST	empecé I began	empezó one subject began	empezamos we began	empezaron two or more subjects began
IMPERFECT PAST	empezaba I began	empezaba one subject began	empezabámos we began	empezaban two or more subjects began
BELIEVE = CREER*				
PRESENT	creo I believe	cree one subject believes	creemos we believe	creen two or more subjects believe
PRETERITE PAST	creí I believed	creyó one subject believed	creímos we believed	creyeron two or more subjects believed
IMPERFECT PAST	creía I believed	creía one subject believed	creíamos we believed	creían two or more subjects believed
BRING = TRAER*				
PRESENT	traigo I bring	trae one subject brings	traemos we bring	traen two or more subjects bring
PRETERITE PAST	traje I brought	trajo one subject brought	trajimos we brought	trajeron two or more subjects brought
IMPERFECT PAST	traía I used to bring	traía one subject used to bring	traíamos we used to bring	traían two or more used to bring
BUY = COMPRAR				
PRESENT	compro I buy	compra one subject buys	compramos we buy	compran two or more subjects buy
PRETERITE PAST	compré I bought	compró one subject bought	compramos we bought	compraron two or more subjects bought
IMPERFECT PAST	compraba I used to buy	compraba one subject used to buy	comprábamos we used to buy	compraban two or more subjects used to buy
CALL (BE CALLED / BE NAMED) = LLAMAR(SE)				
PRESENT	llamo (me llamo) I call (am named)	llama (se llama) one calls (is named)	llamamos (nos llamamos) we call (are named)	llaman (se llaman) two or more call (are named)
PRETERITE PAST	llamé (me llamé) I called (was named)	llamó se llamó one called (was named)	llamamos nos llamamos we called (were named)	llamaron se llamaron two or more called (were named)
IMPERFECT PAST	llamaba me llamaba I called (was named)	llamaba se llamaba one called (was named)	llamabámos nos llamabámos we called (were named)	llamaban se llamaban two or more called (were named)

VERB TABLE 116	YO = I	ELLA / ÉL / USTED = SHE / HE / YOU	NOSOTROS = WE	YOU PLURAL / THEY = USTEDES / ELLOS
CAN / BE ABLE = PODER*				
PRESENT	puedo I can / am able	puede one subject can / is able	podemos we can / are able	pueden two or more can / are able
PRETERITE PAST	pude I could / was able	pudo one subject was able	pudimos we were able	pudieron two or more subjects were able
IMPERFECT PAST	podía I could	podía one subject could	podíamos we could	podían two or more subjects could
CARRY / WEAR / TAKE AWAY = LLEVAR				
PRESENT	llevo I carry / wear / take away	lleva one subject carries / wears / takes away	llevamos we carry / wear / take away	llevan two or more subjects carry / wear / take away
PRETERITE PAST	llevé I carried / wore / took away	llevé one subject carried / wore / took away	llevamos we carried / wore / took away	llevaron two or more subjects carried / wore / took away
IMPERFECT PAST	llevaba I carried / wore / took away	llevaba one subject carried / wore / took away	llevábamos we carried / wore / took away	llevaban two or more subjects carried / wore / took away
CLOSE = CERRAR*				
PRESENT	cierro I close	cierra one subject closes	cerramos we close	cierran two or more subjects close
PRETERITE PAST	cerré I closed	cerró one subject closed	cerramos we closed	cerraron two or more subjects closed
IMPERFECT PAST	cerraba I closed	cerraba one subject closed	cerrábamos we closed	cerraban two or more subjects closed
COME = VENIR*				
PRESENT	vengo I come	viene one subject comees	venimos we come	vienen two or more subjects come
PRETERITE PAST	vine I came	vino one subject came	vinimos we came	vinieron two or more subjects came
IMPERFECT PAST	venía I came	venía one subject came	veníamos we came	venían two or more subjects came
COOK = COCINAR				
PRESENT	cocino I cook	cocina one subject cooks	cocinamos we cook	cocinan two or more subjects cook
PRETERITE PAST	cociné I cooked	cocinó one subject cooked	cocinamos we cooked	cocinaron two or more subjects cooked
IMPERFECT PAST	cocinaba I cooked	cocinaba one subject cooked	cocinábamos we cooked	cocinaban two or more subjects cooked

* an irregular verb

SPANISH CHATBOOK ❷   © SPANISH CHAT COMPANY

VERB TABLE 117	YO = I	ELLA / ÉL / USTED = SHE / HE / YOU	NOSOTROS = WE	YOU PLURAL / THEY = USTEDES / ELLOS
COUNT / TELL A STORY = CONTAR*				
PRESENT	cuento I count / tell a story	cuenta one counts / tells a story	contamos we count / tell a story	cuentan two or more count / tell a story
PRETERITE PAST	conté I counted / told a story	contó one counted / told a story	contamos we counted / told a story	contaron two or more counted / told a story
IMPERFECT PAST	contaba I counted / told a story	contaba one counted / told a story	contábamos we counted / told a story	contaban two or more counted / told a story
DO / MAKE = HACER*				
PRESENT	hago I do / make	hace one subject does / makes	hicimos we do / make	hacen two or more subjects do / make
PRETERITE PAST	hice I did / made	hizo one subject did / made	hicimos we did / made	hicieron two or more subjects did / made
IMPERFECT PAST	hacía I did / made	hacía one subject did / made	hacíamos we did / made	hacían two or more subjects did / made
DRINK = BEBER				
PRESENT	bebo I drink	bebe one subject drinks	bebemos we drink	beben two or more subjects drink
PRETERITE PAST	bebí I drank	bebió one subject drank	bebimos we drank	bebieron two or more subjects drank
IMPERFECT PAST	bebía I drank	bebía one subject drank	bebíamos we drank	bebían two or more subjects drank
EAT = COMER				
PRESENT	como I eat	come one subject eats	comemos we eat	comen two or more subjects eat
PRETERITE PAST	comí I ate	comió one subject ate	comimos we ate	comieron two or more subjects ate
IMPERFECT PAST	comía I ate	comía one subject ate	comíamos we ate	comían two or more subjects ate
ENJOY (ENJOY ONESELF) = DIVERTIR(SE)*				
PRESENT	(me) diverto I enjoy myself	(se) diverte one subject enjoys / has a good time	(nos) divertimos we enjoy ourselves	(se) divierten two or more subjects enjoys / have a good time
PRETERITE PAST	(me) divertí I enjoyed myself	(se) divirtió one had a good time	(nos) divertimos we enjoyed ourselves	(se) divirtieron two or more had a good time
IMPERFECT PAST	(me) divertía I enjoyed myself	(se) divertía one had a good time	(nos) divertíamos we enjoyed ourselves	(se) divertían two or more had a good time

© SPANISH CHAT COMPANY

VERB TABLE 118	YO = I	ELLA / ÉL / USTED = SHE / HE / YOU	NOSOTROS = WE	YOU PLURAL / THEY = USTEDES / ELLOS
FALL (DOWN) = CAER(SE)				
PRESENT	(me) caigo I fall (down)	(se) cae one subject falls (down)	(nos) caemos we fall (down)	(se) caen two or more subjects fall (down)
PRETERITE PAST	(me) caí I fell (down)	(se) cayó one subject fell (down)	(nos) caímos we fell (down)	(se) cayeron two or more fell (down)
IMPERFECT PAST	(me) caía I fell (down)	(se) caía one subject fell (down)	(nos) caíamos we fell (down)	(se) caían two or more fell (down)
FEEL (FEEL EMOTIONS / HEALTH) = SENTIR (SE)*				
PRESENT	(me) siento I feel (emotions / health)	(se) siente one subject feels (emotions / health)	(nos) sentimos we feel (emotions / health)	(se) sienten two or more subjects feel (emotions / health)
PRETERITE PAST	(me) sentí I felt (emotions / health)	(se) sintió one subject felt (emotions / health)	(nos) sentimos we felt	(se) sintieron two or more subjects felt (emotions / health)
IMPERFECT PAST	(me) sentía I felt (emotions / health)	(se) sentía one subject felt (emotions / health)	(nos) sentíamos we felt (emotions / health)	(se) sentían two or more subjects felt (emotions / health)
FIND = ENCONTRAR*				
PRESENT	encuentro I find	encuentra one subject finds	encontramos we find	encuentran two or more subjects find
PRETERITE PAST	encontré I found	encontró one subject found	encontramos we found	encontraron two or more subjects found
IMPERFECT PAST	encontraba I found	encontraba one subject found	encontrábamos we found	encontraban two or more subjects found
FINISH / END = TERMINAR				
PRESENT	termino I finish	termina one subject finishes	terminamos we finish	terminan two or more subjects finish
PRETERITE PAST	terminé I finished	terminó one subjects finished	terminamos we finished	terminaron two or more subjects finished
IMPERFECT PAST	terminaba I finished	terminaba one subjects finished	terminábamos we finished	terminaban two or more subjects finished
GIVE = DAR*				
PRESENT	doy I give	da one subject gives	damos we give	dan two or more subjects give
PRETERITE PAST	di I gave	dio one subject gave	dimos we gave	dieron two or more subjects gave
IMPERFECT PAST	daba I gave	daba one subject gave	dábamos we gave	daban two or more subjects gave

VERB TABLE 119	YO = I	ELLA / ÉL / USTED = SHE / HE / YOU	NOSOTROS = WE	YOU PLURAL / THEY = USTEDES / ELLOS
GO (GO ONESELF) / GO TO = IR (SE) / IR A*				
PRESENT	voy / (me) voy a I go / am going to	va / (se) va a one goes / is going to	vamos/(nos)vamos a we go / are going to	van / (se) van a two or more go / were going to
PRETERITE PAST	fui / (me) fui a I went / was going to	fue / (se) fue a one went / was going to	fuimos/(nos)fuimos a we went / were going to	fueron / (se) fueron a two or more went / were going to
IMPERFECT PAST	iba / (me) iba a I went / was going to	iba / (se) iba a one went / was going to	íbamos / (nos) íbamos a we went / were going to	iban / (se) iban a two or more went / were going to
HAVE / HOLD = TENER*				
PRESENT	tengo I have / hold	tiene one subject has / holds	tenemos we have / hold	tienen two or more subjects have / hold
PRETERITE PAST	tuve I held / received	tuvo one subject held /received	tuvimos we held / received	tuvieron two or more held /received
IMPERFECT PAST	tenía I had	tenía one subject had	teníamos we had	tenían two or more had
HURT(COMPLAIN ABOUT / REGRET) = DOLER(SE)*				
PRESENT	(me) duele I hurt	(se) duele one subject hurts	(nos) dolemos we hurt	(se) duelen two or more subjects hurt
PRETERITE PAST	(me) dolí I hurt	(se) dolió one subject hurt	(nos) dolimos we hurt	(se) dolieron two or more subjects hurt
IMPERFECT PAST	(me) dolía I hurt	(se) dolía one subject hurt	(nos) dolíamos we hurt	(se) dolían two or more subjects hurt
KNOW INFORMATION = SABER*				
PRESENT	sé I know	sabe one subject knows	sabemos we know	saben two or more subjects know
PRETERITE PAST	supe I found out	supo one subject found out	supimos we found out	supieron two or more subjects found out
IMPERFECT PAST	sabía I knew	sabía one subject knew	sabíamos we knew	sabían two or more subjects knew
KNOW / BE ACQUAINTED WITH SOMEONE / SOMEPLACE = CONOCER*				
PRESENT	conozco I know	conoce one subject knows	conocemos we know	conocen two or more subjects know
PRETERITE PAST	conocí I met	conoció one subject met	conocimos we met	conocieron two or more subjects met
IMPERFECT PAST	conocía I knew	conocía one subject knew	conocíamos we knew	conocían two or more subjects knew

* an irregular verb

VERB TABLE 120

	YO = I	ELLA / ÉL / USTED = SHE / HE / YOU	NOSOTROS = WE	YOU PLURAL / THEY = USTEDES / ELLOS
LEARN = APRENDER				
PRESENT	aprendo I learn	aprende one subject learns	aprendemos we learn	aprenden two or more subjects learn
PRETERITE PAST	aprendí I learned	aprendió one subject learned	aprendimos we learned	aprendieron two or more subjects learned
IMPERFECT PAST	aprendía I learned	aprendía one subject learned	aprendíamos we learned	aprendían two or more subjects learned
LEAVE = SALIR*				
PRESENT	salgo I leave	sale one subject leaves	salimos we leave	salen two or more subjects leave
PRETERITE PAST	salí I left	salió one subject left	salimos we left	salieron two or more subjects left
IMPERFECT PAST	salía I left	salía one subject left	salíamos we left	salían two or more subjects left
LIKE = GUSTAR* (USE GUSTAN BEFORE PLURAL NOUNS)				
PRESENT	me gusta (n) I like	le gusta (n) one subject likes	nos gusta (n) we like	les gusta (n) two or more subjects like
PRETERITE PAST	me gustó (me gustaron) I liked	le gustó (le gustaron) one subject liked	nos gustó (nos gustaron) we liked	les gustó (les gustaron) two or more subjects liked
IMPERFECT PAST	me gustaba (n) I liked	le gustaba (n) one subject liked	nos gustaba (n) we liked	les gustaba (n) two or more subjects liked
LIVE = VIVIR*				
PRESENT	vivo I live	vive one subject lives	vivimos we live	viven two or more subjects live
PRETERITE PAST	viví I lived	vivió one subject lived	vivimos we lived	vivieron two or more subjects lived
IMPERFECT PAST	vivía I lived	vivía one subject lived	vivíamos we lived	vivían two or more subjects lived
LOSE = PERDER*				
PRESENT	pierdo I lose	pierde one subject loses	perdemos we lose	pierden two or more subjects lose
PRETERITE PAST	perdí I lost	perdió one subject lost	perdimos we lost	perdieron two or more subjects lost
IMPERFECT PAST	perdía I lost	perdía one subject lost	perdíamos we lost	perdían two or more subjects lost

VERB TABLE 121	YO = I	ELLA / ÉL / USTED = SHE / HE / YOU	NOSOTROS = WE	YOU PLURAL / THEY = USTEDES / ELLOS
NEED = NECESITAR				
PRESENT	necesito I need	necesita one subject needs	necesitamos we need	necesitan two or more subjects need
PRETERITE PAST	necesité I needed	necesitó one subject needed	necesitamos we needed	necesitaron two or more subjects needed
IMPERFECT PAST	necesitaba I needed	necesitaba one subject needed	necesitábamos we needed	necesitaban two or more subjects needed
OPEN = ABRIR				
PRESENT	abro I open	abre one subject opens	abrimos we open	abren two or more subjects open
PRETERITE PAST	abrí I opened	abrió one subject opened	abrimos we opened	abrieron two or more subjects opened
IMPERFECT PAST	abría I opened	abría one subject opened	abríamos we opened	abrían two or more subjects opened
OWE / SHOULD / BE OBLIGATED = DEBER				
PRESENT	debo I owe / should	debe one owes / should	debemos we owe / should	deben two or more owe / should
PRETERITE PAST	debí I owed / must have	debió one owed / must have	debimos we owed / must have	debieron two or more owed / must have
IMPERFECT PAST	debía I owed / should	debía one owed / should	debíamos we owed / should	debían two or more owed / should
PAY = PAGAR				
PRESENT	pago I pay	paga one subject pays	pagamos we pay	pagan two or more subjects pay
PRETERITE PAST	pagué I paid	pagó one subject paid	pagamos we paid	pagaron two or more subjects paid
IMPERFECT PAST	pagaba I paid	pagaba one subject paid	pagábamos we paid	pagaban two or more subjects paid
PLAY A GAME OR SPORT = JUGAR*				
PRESENT	juego I play	juega one subject plays	jugamos we play	juegan two or more subjects play
PRETERITE PAST	jugué I played	jugó one subject played	jugamos we played	jugaron two or more subjects played
IMPERFECT PAST	jugaba I played	jugaba one subject played	jugábamos we played	jugaban two or more subjects played

* an irregular verb

VERB TABLE 122

	YO = I	ELLA / ÉL / USTED = SHE / HE / YOU	NOSOTROS = WE	YOU PLURAL / THEY = USTEDES / ELLOS
PREFER = PREFERIR*				
PRESENT	prefiero I prefer	prefiere one subject prefer	preferimos we prefer	prefieren two or more subjects prefer
PRETERITE PAST	preferí I preferred	prefirió one subject preferred	preferimos we preferred	prefirieron two or more subjects preferred
IMPERFECT PAST	prefería I preferred	prefería one subject preferred	preferíamos we preferred	preferían two or more subjects preferred
PUT (PUT ON) / BECOME = PONER(SE)*				
PRESENT	(me) pongo I put (put on) / become	(se) pone one puts (puts on) / becomes	(nos) ponemos we put (put on) / become	(se) ponen two or more put (put on) / become
PRETERITE PAST	(me) puse I put (put on) / became	(se) puso one puts (on) / became	(nos) pusimos we put (put on) / became	(se) pusieron two or more put (on) / became
IMPERFECT PAST	(me) ponía I put (put on) / became	(se) ponía one puts (on) / became	(nos) poníamos we put (put on) / became	(se) ponían two or more put (on) / became
READ = LEER*				
PRESENT	leo I read	lee one subject reads	leemos we read	leen two or more subjects read
PRETERITE PAST	leí I read	leyó one subject read	leímos we read	leyeron two or more subjects read
IMPERFECT PAST	leía I read	leía one subject read	leíamos we read	leían two or more subjects read
RECEIVE = RECIBIR				
PRESENT	recibo I receive	recibe one subject receives	recibimos we receive	reciben two or more subjects receive
PRETERITE PAST	recibí I received	recibió one subject received	recibimos we received	recibieron two or more subjects received
IMPERFECT PAST	recibía I received	recibía one subject received	recibíamos we received	recibían two or more subjects received
RECOMMEND = RECOMENDAR*				
PRESENT	recomiendo I recommend	recomienda one subject recommends	recomendamos we recommend	recomiendan two or more recommend
PRETERITE PAST	recomendé I recommended	recomendó one recommended	recomendamos we recommended	recomendaron two or more recommended
IMPERFECT PAST	recomendaba I recommended	recomendaba one recommended	recomendábamos we recommended	recomendaban two or more recommended

SPANISH CHATBOOK 2

VERB TABLE 123

	YO = I	ELLA / ÉL / USTED = SHE / HE / YOU	NOSOTROS = WE	YOU PLURAL / THEY = USTEDES / ELLOS
REMEMBER = RECORDAR*				
PRESENT	recuerdo I remember	recuerda one subject remembers	recordamos we remember	recuerdan two or more subjects remember
PRETERITE PAST	recordé I remembered	recordó one subject remembered	recordamos we remembered	recordaron two or more subjects remembered
IMPERFECT PAST	recordaba I remembered	recordaba one subject remembered	recordábamos we remembered	recordaban two or more subjects remembered
REPEAT = REPETIR*				
PRESENT	repito I repeat	repite one subject repeats	repetimos we repeat	repiten two or more subjects repeat
PRETERITE PAST	repetí I repeated	repitió one subject repeated	repetimos we repeated	repitieron two or more subjects repeated
IMPERFECT PAST	repetía I repeated	repetía one subject repeated	repetíamos we repeated	repetían two or more subjects repeated
RETURN = VOLVER*				
PRESENT	vuelvo I return	vuelve one subject returns	volvemos we return	vuelven two or more subjects return
PRETERITE PAST	volví I returned	volvió one subject returned	volvimos we returned	volvieron two or more subjects returned
IMPERFECT PAST	volvía I returned	volvía one subject returned	volvíamos we returned	volvían two or more subjects returned
SAY / TELL = DECIR*				
PRESENT	digo I say / tell	dice one subject says / tells	decimos we say / tell	dicen two or more subjects say / tell
PRETERITE PAST	dije I said / told	dijo one subject said / told	dijimos we said / told	dijeron two or more subjects said / told
IMPERFECT PAST	decía I said / told	decía one subject said / told	decíamos we said / told	decían two or more subjects said / told
SEE = VER*				
PRESENT	veo I see	ve one subject sees	vemos we see	ven two or more subjects see
PRETERITE PAST	vi I saw	vio one subject saw	vimos we saw	vieron two or more subjects saw
IMPERFECT PAST	veía I saw	veía one subject saw	veíamos we saw	veían two or more subjects saw

* an irregular verb

VERB TABLE 124

	YO = I	ELLA / ÉL / USTED = SHE / HE / YOU	NOSOTROS = WE	YOU PLURAL / THEY = USTEDES / ELLOS
SELL = VENDER				
PRESENT	vendo — I sell	vende — one subject sells	vendemos — we sell	venden — two or more subjects sell
PRETERITE PAST	vendí — I sold	vendió — one subject sold	vendimos — we sold	vendieron — two or more subjects sold
IMPERFECT PAST	vendía — I sold	vendía — one subject sold	vendíamos — we sold	vendían — two or more subjects sold
SLEEP = DORMIR*				
PRESENT	duermo — I sleep	duerme — one subject sleeps	dormimos — we sleep	duermen — two or more subjects sleep
PRETERITE PAST	dormí — I slept	durmió — one subject slept	dormimos — we slept	durmieron — two or more subjects slept
IMPERFECT PAST	dormía — I slept	dormía — one subject slept	dormíamos — we slept	dormían — two or more subjects slept
STAY / REMAIN = QUEDAR (SE)				
PRESENT	(me) quedo — I stay / remain	(se) queda — one subject stays / remains	(nos) quedamos — we stay / remain	(se) quedan — two or more subjects stay / remain
PRETERITE PAST	(me) quedé — I stayed / remained	(se) quedó — one stayed / remained	(nos) quedamos — we stayed / remained	(se) quedaron — two or more stayed / remained
IMPERFECT PAST	(me) quedaba — I stayed / remained	(se) quedaba — one stayed / remained	(nos) quedábamos — we stayed / remained	(se) quedaban — two or more stayed / remained
STUDY = ESTUDIAR				
PRESENT	estudio — I study	estudia — one subject studies	estudiamos — we study	estudian — two or more subjects study
PRETERITE PAST	estudié — I studied	estudió — one subject studied	estudiamos — we studied	estudiaron — two or more subjects studied
IMPERFECT PAST	estudiaba — I studied	estudiaba — one subject studied	estudiábamos — we studied	estudiaban — two or more subjects studied
TALK / SPEAK = HABLAR				
PRESENT	hablo — I talk / speak	habla — one subject talks / speaks	hablamos — we talk / speak	hablan — two or more subjects talk / speak
PRETERITE PAST	hablé — I talked / spoke	habló — one talked / spoke	hablamos — we talked / spoke	hablaron — two or more talked / spoke
IMPERFECT PAST	hablaba — I talked / spoke	hablaba — one talked / spoke	hablábamos — we talked / spoke	hablaban — two or more talked / spoke

SPANISH CHATBOOK 2 © SPANISH CHAT COMPANY

VERB TABLE 125	YO = I	ELLA / ÉL / USTED = SHE / HE / YOU	NOSOTROS = WE	YOU PLURAL / THEY = USTEDES / ELLOS
THINK = PENSAR*				
PRESENT	pienso — I think	piensa — one subject thinks	pensamos — we think	piensan — two or more subjects think
PRETERITE PAST	pensé — I thought	pensó — one subject thought	pensamos — we thought	pensaron — two or more subjects thought
IMPERFECT PAST	pensaba — I thought	pensaba — one subject thought	pensábamos — we thought	pensaban — two or more subjects thought
UNDERSTAND = ENTENDER*				
PRESENT	entiendo — I understand	entiende — one subject understands	entendemos — we understand	entienden — two or more subjects understand
PRETERITE PAST	entendí — I understood	entendió — one subject understood	entendimos — we understood	entendieron — two or more understood
IMPERFECT PAST	entendía — I understood	entendía — one subject understood	entendíamos — we understood	entendían — two or more understood
WANT = QUERER*				
PRESENT	quiero — I want	quiere — one subject wants	queremos — we want	quieren — two or more subjects want
PRETERITE PAST	quise / no quise — I tried / refused	quiso / no quiso — one subject tried / refused	quisimos / no quisimos — we tried / refused	quisieron / no quisieron — two or more subjects tried / refused
IMPERFECT PAST	quería — I wanted	quería — one subject wanted	queríamos — we wanted	querían — two or more subjects wanted
WORK = TRABAJAR				
PRESENT	trabajo — I work	trabaja — one subject works	trabajamos — we work	trabajan — two or more subjects work
PRETERITE PAST	trabajé — I worked	trabajó — one subject worked	trabajamos — we worked	trabajaron — two or more subjects worked
IMPERFECT PAST	trabajaba — I worked	trabajaba — one subject worked	trabajábamos — we worked	trabajaban — two or more subjects worked
WRITE = ESCRIBIR				
PRESENT	escribo — I write	escribe — one subject writes	escribimos — we write	escriben — two or more subjects write
PRETERITE PAST	escribí — I wrote	escribió — one subject wrote	escribimos — we wrote	escribíamos — two or more subjects wrote
IMPERFECT PAST	escribía — I wrote	escribía — one subject wrote	escribíamos — we wrote	escribían — two or more subjects wrote

* an irregular verb

LAS RESPUESTAS | ANSWER KEY

LAS RESPUESTAS ESTÁN AQUÍ. =

The answers are here.

RESPUESTAS = ANSWERS

LECCIÓN 1 — **12** DOCE

IDEAS PARA LAS FRASES = IDEAS FOR SENTENCES

HABLAR = to talk / to speak	yo hablo... = I speak usted habla... = you speak ustedes hablan... = you all speak	por teléfono = by phone mucho Inglés = a lot of English un poco de Español = a little Spanish sobre mi / su tarea = about my/ (his/her) homework en voz alto = in a loud voice en voz bajo = in a quiet voice más despacio = more slowly con la directora = with the principal
TRABAJAR = to work	yo trabajo... = I work usted trabaja... = you work ustedes trabajan.. = you all work	en la compañía Spanish Chat = for Spanish Chat Company en una oficina = in an office en una escuela = in a school como asistente = as an assistent como profesor(a) = as a teacher como mesera(o)= as a server como gerente = as a manager demasiado = too much con mi hermana(o) = with my sister(brother)
EMPEZAR* = to start / to begin *the stem changes from -e- to -ie-	yo empiezo... = I start usted empieza... = you start ellos empiezan... = they start	a las seis (de la mañana) = at 6 a.m. (in the morning) mi trabajo = my job a trabajar = to work muy tarde = very late temprano = early con la página 1 = with (the) page 1
TERMINAR = to finish / to end	yo termino... = I finish usted termina... = you finish ellos terminan... = they finish	a la una y media de la tarde = at 1:30 in the afternoon a las diez de la noche = at 10:00 at night la tarea para la clase = the homework for the class el examen = the test mi trabajo / su trabajo = my job / your job de comer = to eat (the English would be eating) mis / sus quehaceres = my / your housework rápidamente = quickly

RESPUESTAS = ANSWERS

LECCIÓN 1 — **14** CATORCE

1. La niña,
2. Una niña
3. El niño
4. Un niño
5. Las estudiantes
6. Unas (algunas) estudiantes
7. Los primos....los hoteles,
8. Unos (algunos) primos...unos (algunos) hoteles

RESPUESTAS = ANSWERS

LECCIÓN 1 — 15 QUINCE

LUGARES = PLACES
3. FALSE They were fictional characters written by Cervantes in 1605 so they do not currently "work" in Barcelona.

DÍAS FESTIVOS = HOLIDAYS
2. FALSE They throw tomatoes, not grapes during "La Tomatina."

RESPUESTAS = ANSWERS

LECCIÓN 1 — 17 DIECISIETE

1. ¿Termina su hija con la comida? = <u>Finish your daughter (Is your daughter finished) with the food?</u>

2. Ellos hablan un poco de Inglés. = <u>They speak a little English.</u>

3. Yo trabajo cada día. = <u>I work every day.</u>

4. Él termina la tarjeta de invitación para la fiesta. = <u>He finishes the invitation card for the party.</u>

5. ¿A qué hora empieza su escuela? = <u>When (does) her school begin?</u>

6. Yo hablo por teléfono en mi oficina. = <u>I talk on the telephone in my office.</u>

7. They finish their work. = <u>Ellos terminan su trabajo.</u>

8. Do you speak Spanish? = <u>¿Habla usted español?</u>

9. Where do you all work? = <u>¿Dónde trabajan ustedes?</u>

10. I begin to work at the house. = <u>Yo empiezo a trabajar en la casa.</u>

11. My son works at the museum = <u>Mi hijo trabaja en el museo.</u>

12. When do they begin? = <u>¿Cuándo empiezan ellos?</u>

RESPUESTAS = ANSWERS

LECCIÓN 1
18 DIECIOCHO

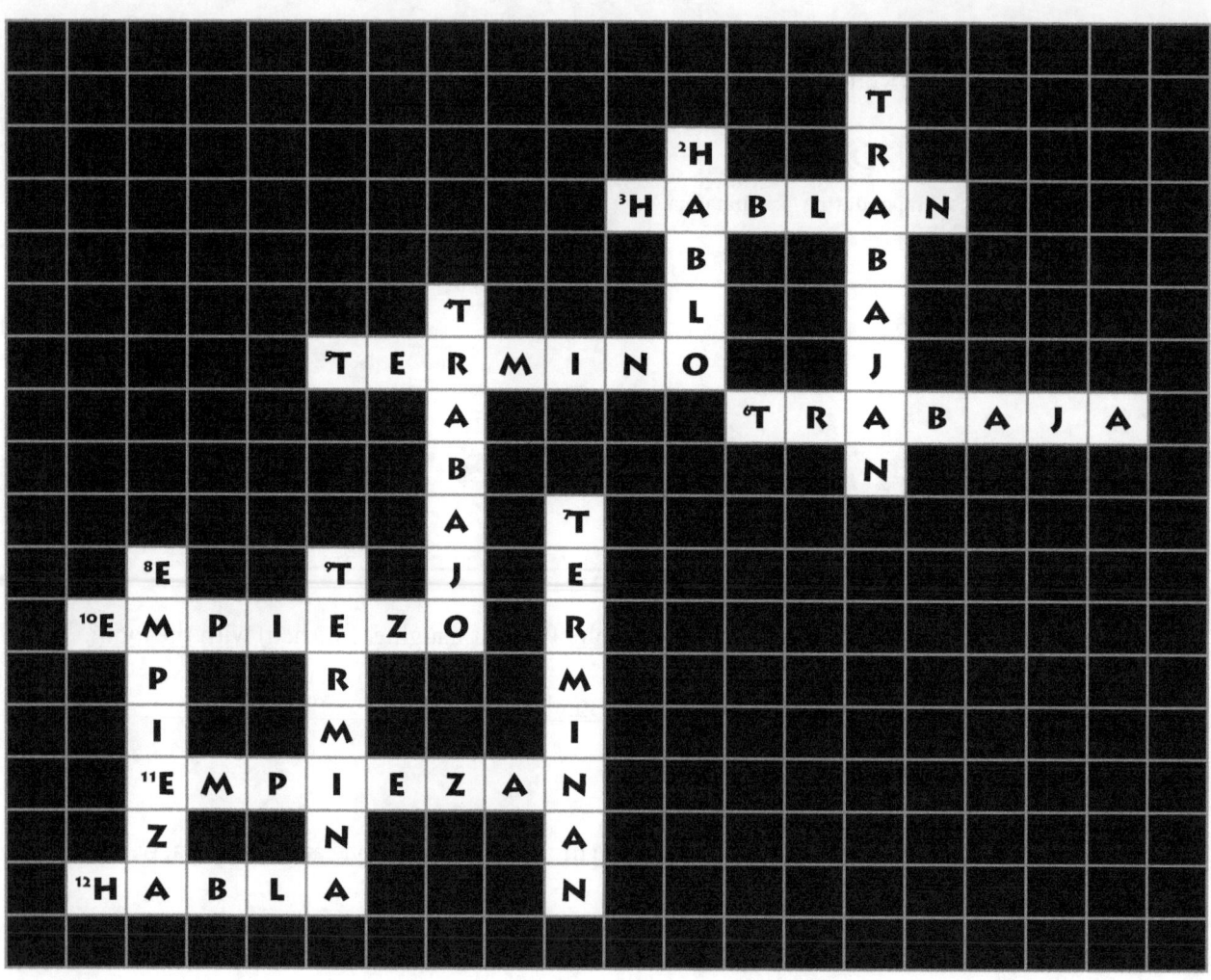

HORIZONTAL

3 they talk = **ellos hablan**

5 I finish = **yo termino**

6 he works = **él trabaja**

10 I begin = **yo empiezo**

11 you all begin = **ustedes empiezan**

12 she talks = **ella habla**

VERTICAL

1 they work = **ellos trabajan**

2 I speak = **yo hablo**

4 I work = **yo trabajo**

7 you all finish = **ustedes terminan**

8 you begin = **usted empieza**

9 you finish = **usted termina**

RESPUESTAS = ANSWERS

LECCIÓN 2

IDEAS PARA LAS FRASES =		IDEAS FOR SENTENCES
VIVIR = to live	**yo vivo...** = I live **usted vive...** = you live **ustedes viven...** = you all live	**en Omaha, Nebraska** = in Omaha, Nebraska **en los Estados Unidos de América** = In the U.S.A. **en una casa grande** = in a big house **en un apartamento pequeño** = in a small apartment **sola(o)** = alone or by myself **con mi familia** = with my family
COMER = to eat	**yo como...** = I eat **usted come...** = you eat **ustedes comen...** = you all eat	**suficientes verduras** = enough vegetables **muchas frutas** = many fruits **dulces cada día** = sweets each day **naranjas para el desayuno** = oranges for breakfast **ensalada para el almuerzo** = salad for lunch **hamburguesa para la cena** = hamburger for dinner **zanahorias para una merienda** = carrots for a snack **sopa de tomate** = tomato soup **coliflor y brócoli** = cauliflower and broccoli
QUERER* = to want / to wish *the stem changes from -e- to -ie-*	**yo quiero...** = I want / I wish **usted quiere...** = you want / wish **ustedes quieren...** = you all want / wish	**viajar a América del Sur** = travel to South America **viajar a la ciudad de Panamá** = travel to Panama City **visitar las montañas** = visit the mountains **visitar a mi familia** = visit my family **ir a un hotel** = go to a hotel **ir a la playa** = go to the beach **ir al campo** = go to the countryside **comer más frutas y verduras** = eat more fruit & vegetables **mucho dinero** = a lot of money
TENER* = to have *the stem changes from -e- to -ie- and the "yo" form is "tengo"*	**yo tengo..** = I have **usted tiene...** = you have **ellos tienen...** = they have	**dos hermanos mayores** = two older siblings **tres hermanas menores** = three younger sisters **una hermana mayor** = an older sister **un hermano menor** = a younger brother **seis hijos** = six children **once sobrinos** = eleven nieces and nephews **perros y gatos** = dogs and cats **hambre y sed** = hunger and thirst

RESPUESTAS = ANSWERS

LECCIÓN 2

1. algo
2. nada
3. siempre
4. nunca
5. alguien
6. nadie
7. tampoco
8. ni...ni

RESPUESTAS = ANSWERS

LECCIÓN 2 — 25 VEINTICINCO

LUGARES = PLACES
1. FALSE No one lives on the Teotihuacán Avenida de los Muertos = Avenue of the Dead, there is no such thing as the "Avenida de las Almas Vivas."

DÍAS FESTIVOS = HOLIDAYS
3. FALSE Las Posadas is celebrated is only celebrated for nine days, not 12.

RESPUESTAS = ANSWERS

LECCIÓN 2 — 27 VEINTISIETE

1. Ustedes viven en los Estados Unidos de América. = <u>You all live in the U.S.A.</u>

2. ¿Nadie quiere comer sus verduras? = <u>No one wants to eat their vegetables?</u>

3. ¿Tienen ustedes algunas clases en la universidad? = <u>(Do) you all have some classes at the University?</u>

4. Él nunca come arroz con pollo para su almuerzo. = <u>He never eats rice with chicken for his lunch.</u>

5. Yo tengo mucha tarea. = <u>I have a lot of homework.</u>

6. ¿Vive usted cerca de alguna amiga? = <u>(Do) you live close to some female friend?</u>

7. My dogs always eat a lot. = <u>Mis perros siempre comen mucho.</u>

8. I also do not live with my grandparents. = <u>Yo tampoco vivo con mis abuelos.</u>

9. I want to work tomorrow also. = <u>Quiero trabajar mañana también.</u>

10. You all want to eat something? = <u>¿Quieren ustedes comer algo?</u>

11. The family has dessert at 9 p.m. = <u>La familia tiene postre a las nueve de la tarde.</u>

12. I never eat nothing for breakfast. = <u>Yo nunca como nada para el desayuno.</u>

RESPUESTAS = ANSWERS

LECCIÓN 2
28 VEINTIOCHO

BUSCAPALABRAS = WORD SEARCH

1. he lives = **él vive**
2. I have = **yo tengo**
3. they want = **ellos quieren**
4. you all eat = **ustedes comen**
5. she wants = **ella quiere**
6. I live = **yo vivo**
7. you have = **usted tiene**
8. I eat = **yo como**
9. I want = **yo quiero**
10. he eats = **él come**
11. they have = **ellos tienen**
12. you all live = **ustedes viven**

RESPUESTAS = ANSWERS

LECCIÓN 3
32 TREINTA Y DOS

IDEAS PARA LAS FRASES = IDEAS FOR SENTENCES

IR* = to go *memorize this one	**yo voy...** = I go **usted va...** = you go **ustedes van...** = you all go	**a la ciudad de Nueva York** = to New York City **a las montañas** = to the mountains **a mi cuarto para leer un libro** = to my room to read a book **a la playa** = to the beach **al campo** = to the countryside **al lago** = to the lake **al río** = to the river
VER* = to see *the stem is the letter "V" the "yo" form is "veo".	**yo veo...** = I see **usted ve...** = you see **ustedes ven...** = you all see	**el reloj y son las dos de la tarde** = the clock and it is 2:00 p.m. **a mis primos** = my cousins **a mi tío y tía** = my aunt and uncle **a mis cuñados** = my sister-in-law and brother-in-law **a sus suegros** = her mother-in-law and father-in-law **a mi nuera y mi yerno** = my daughter-in law and son-in-law **a mi esposo / mi esposa** = my husband / my wife
ESTAR* = to be (changing) *the "yo" form is "estoy" add accents to "está" and "están"	**yo estoy...** = I am **usted está...** = you are **ustedes están...** = you all are	**bien / no muy bien** = well / not very well **cansada(o)** = tired (female/male) **enferma(o)** = sick (female/male) **en frente** = in front of **atrás** = behind **aquí / allí / allá** = here / there / way over there **derecho por el pasillo** = straight down the hall **a la izquierda** = on the left **a la derecha** = on the right
SER* = to be (permanent) *memorize this one	**yo soy...** = I am **usted es...** = you are **ustedes son...** = you all are	**de los Estados Unidos de América** = from the U.S.A **alta(o) / baja(o)** = tall / short (female/male) **rubia(o) / morena(o)** = blond / brunette (female/male) **un(a) buen(a) trabajador(a)** = a good worker **un(a) mesera(o)** = a server (female/male) **la dueña / el dueño** = the owner (female/male)

RESPUESTAS = ANSWERS

LECCIÓN 3
34 TREINTA Y CUATRO

1. mi
2. mía
3. su
4. suyos (you already have the **los** before the word **equipos**)
5. nuestros
6. nuestras

RESPUESTAS = ANSWERS

LECCIÓN 3
35 TREINTA Y CINCO

LUGARES = PLACES
2. FALSE It takes eight to 10 hours to pass through the Panama canal.

DÍAS FESTIVOS = HOLIDAYS
1. FALSE On September 15, you can find an Independence day "fiesta = celebration" at any of the Central American countries except for Panama because their Independence day is November 28th. An interesting fact is that the news of Independence from Spain did not reach Mexico City (North America) until one day later and that is why they celebrate on September 16.

RESPUESTAS = ANSWERS

LECCIÓN 3
37 TREINTA Y SIETE

A For a porter it is not hard to lift a lot of luggage up the tall stairs.
(ah)

B The girls are great dancers with their flags and their beautiful dresses of many colors.
(beh)

C My poor boss is in bad health.
(seh)

D I am going to change money at the next cashier.
(deh)

E The 15 minute break is to drink a (small) coffee.
(eh)

F They see nice wait staff who receive good tips.
(ehf-feh)

G The passenger is on the airplane.
(heh)

H The travel agents go to many parts of the world.
(ah-cheh)

I The pedestrians are quite possibly in danger with so many cars downtown.
(eee)

J He sees the map at the train station.
(hoh-tah)

C 1. Mi pobre jefe está mal de salud.

G 2. La pasajera está en el avión.

J 3. Él ve el mapa en la estación del tren.

I 4. Los peatones están en posible peligro con tantos carros en el centro.

A 5. Para el portero no es difícil subir mucho equipaje por las escaleras altas.

B 6. Las chicas son buenas bailarinas con sus banderas y sus vestidos bonitos de muchos colores.

D 7. Voy a cambiar dinero en el próximo cajero.

F 8. Ellos ven meseros simpáticos que reciben buenas propinas.

E 9. Los 15 minutos de descanso son para tomar un cafecito.

H 10. Los agentes de viajes van a muchas partes del mundo.

RESPUESTAS = ANSWERS

LECCIÓN 3
38 TREINTA Y OCHO

1. I am tired. (changing) = Yo <u>estoy</u> cansada. E S T O **Y**

2. She goes to the office. = Ella <u>va</u> a la oficina. V **A**

3. I see another way. = Yo <u>veo</u> otra manera. **V** E O

4. They go fast. = Ellos <u>van</u> rápido. V **A** N

5. Nice to meet you. = <u>Mucho</u> gusto. **M** U C H O

6. I am a teacher. = Yo <u>soy</u> una maestra. S **O** Y

7. They are tall. = Ellos <u>son</u> altos. **S** O N

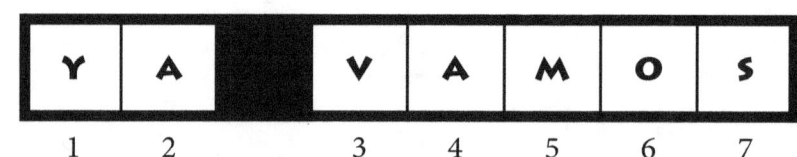

Y	A		V	A	M	O	S
1	2		3	4	5	6	7

SPANISH CHATBOOK ❷ © SPANISH CHAT COMPANY

RESPUESTAS = ANSWERS

LECCIÓN 4
42 CUARENTA Y DOS

IDEAS PARA LAS FRASES = IDEAS FOR SENTENCES

	USE THESE CLUES TO CHOOSE	CONJUGATIONS	POSSIBLE ENDINGS
HABLAR = to talk = *preterite*	**a las seis de la tarde** = at 6 p.m. **anoche** = last night **la semana pasada** = last week	**yo hablé...** = I spoke **usted habló...** = you spoke **ustedes hablaron...** = you all spoke	**con la directora** = with the principal **por teléfono** = by phone **mucho Inglés** = a lot of English **un poco de Español** = a little Spanish **sobre mis/ sus amigos** = about my (his/her) friends
HABLAR = to talk *imperfect*	**a menudo** = often **cada día** = every day **todo el tiempo** = all the time	**yo hablaba...** = I used to speak **usted hablaba...** = you used to speak **ustedes hablaban...** = you all used to speak	
TERMINAR = to finish *preterite*	**antes de ayer** = the day before yesterday **el otro día** = the other day **en ese momento** = at that moment	**yo terminé...** = I finished **usted terminó...** = you finished **ellos terminaron...** = they finished	**con la tarea** = with the homework **el examen** = the test **mi trabajo** = my job **a comer** = to eat (eating) **sus quehaceres** = his/her/your housework **mis estudios** = my studies **un proyecto** = a project
TERMINAR = to finish *imperfect*	**a veces** = sometimes **con frecuencia** = frequently **siempre** = for always	**yo terminaba...** = I used to finish **usted terminaba...** = you used to finish **ellos terminaban...** = they used to finish	
TRABAJAR = to work *preterite*	**el último mes** = the last month **hace un año** = a year ago **a las ocho de la mañana** = at 8 a.m.	**yo trabajé...** = I worked **usted trabajó...** = you worked **ustedes trabajaron...** = you all worked	**en la escuela como maestra** = in the school as a teacher **demasiado** = too much **en Spanish Chat Company** = at Spanish Chat Company **con mi hermana** = with my sister **en un restaurante** = in a restaurant
TRABAJAR = to work *imperfect*	**generalmente** = generally **muchas veces** = many times **mucho** = a lot	**yo trabajaba...** = I used to work **usted trabajaba...** = you used to work **ustedes trabajaban...** = you all used to work	
EMPEZAR* = to begin *preterite* *z changes to c*	**ayer por la tarde** = yesterday afternoon **hace quince años** = 15 years ago **esta mañana** = this morning	**yo empecé...** = I started **usted empezó...** = you started **ellos empezaron...** = they started	**a trabajar** = to work **muy tarde** = very late **temprano** = early **con la página 1** = with page 1 **a jugar tenis** = to play tennis **a hacer ejercicio** = to exercise
EMPEZAR = to begin *imperfect*	**usualmente** = usually **todos los días** = every day **cada semana** = every week	**yo empezaba...** = I used to start **usted empezaba...** = you used to start **ellos empezaban...** = they used to start	

RESPUESTAS = ANSWERS

LECCIÓN 4 — 44 CUARENTA Y CUATRO

1. aquella
2. ese, esos
3. esta
4. aquellas

RESPUESTAS = ANSWERS

LECCIÓN 4 — 45 CUARENTA Y CINCO

LUGARES = PLACES

2. **FALSE** Cartagena is famous for the Colonial area of the city built around 1533.

DÍAS FESTIVOS = HOLIDAYS

1. **FALSE** The National Day of the Liberator is named for Simón Bolívar who as a politician and general helped gain independence for South America from Spain. Many streets throughout Latin America are named Avenida Bolívar or even Calle Bolívar. The country of Bolivia and their money, the Bolivianos, as well as the money of Venezuela, the Bolívar, are all named after Simón.

RESPUESTAS = ANSWERS

LECCIÓN 4 — 47 CUARENTA Y SIETE

1. Hace un mes yo empecé a... = A month ago I began to...
2. Yo empezaba (a)... = I began (to) ...
3. Él siempre empezaba (a)...cuando... = He always began (to) ...when...
4. Después que yo trabajé... = After I worked...
5. Ayer ustedes trabajaron en... = Yesterday you all worked in/on/at...
6. Ustedes trabajaban muchas veces... = You all worked many times in/on/at...
7. Yo terminaba todos los días con... = I end every day with...
8. Anoche ella terminó... = Last night she finished...
9. Ella a veces terminaba sin... = She sometimes ended/ finished without...
10. Esta mañana usted habló (con/en/sobre/a)... = This morning you spoke (with/in/about/to)...
11. La otra semana ellos hablaron... = (The) other week they spoke...
12. Cuando ellos hablaban entonces = When they spoke then...

RESPUESTAS = ANSWERS

LECCIÓN 4
48 CUARENTA Y OCHO

HORIZONTAL (PRETERITE)

2 I began = yo **empecé**

5 I spoke = yo **hablé**

6 the children talked = **los niños hablaron**

8 you worked = **usted trabajó**

10 you all worked = **ustedes trabajaron**

12 Elena & Jaden began = **Elena y Jaden empezaron**

VERTICAL (IMPERFECT)

1 they began = **ellas empezaban**

3 I spoke = yo **hablaba**

4 you all talked = **ustedes hablaban**

7 they worked = **ellos trabjaban**

9 you worked = **usted trabajaba**

11 I finished = yo **terminaba**

© SPANISH CHAT COMPANY

SPANISH CHATBOOK 2

RESPUESTAS = ANSWERS

LECCIÓN 5
52 CINCUENTA Y DOS

IDEAS PARA LAS FRASES = IDEAS FOR SENTENCES

	USE THESE CLUES TO CHOOSE	CONJUGATIONS	POSSIBLE ENDINGS
COMER = to eat *preterite*	**ayer** = yesterday **anoche** = last night **la semana pasada** = last week	**yo comí...** = I ate **usted comió...** = you ate **ustedes comieron...** = you all ate	**carne** = meat **ensalada** = salad **papas** = potatoes **helado** = ice cream **arroz** = rice **pollo** = chicken **galleta** = cookie **demasiado** = too much
COMER = to eat *imperfect*	**a menudo** = often **cada día** = each day **cada semana** = each week	**yo comía...** = I used to eat **usted comía...** = you used to eat **ustedes comían...** = you all used to eat	
VIVIR = to live *preterite*	**antes de ayer** = the day before yesterday **el otro día** = the other day **en ese momento** = at that moment	**yo viví...** = I lived **usted vivió...** = you lived **ellos vivieron...** = they lived	**en Omaha, Nebraska** = in Omaha, Nebraska **en los Estados Unidos de América** = In the U.S.A. **en una casa** = in a house **en un apartamento** = in a apartment **felizmente** = happily
VIVIR = to live *imperfect*	**a veces** = sometimes **con frecuencia** = frequently **siempre** = always	**yo vivía...** = I used to live **usted vivía...** = you used to live **ellos vivían...** = they used to live	
QUERER* = to want/ wish *preterite* *stem-uis*	**el último mes** = the last month **ayer por la mañana** = yesterday morning **hace dos días** = two days ago	**yo quise...** = I wanted **usted quiso...** = you wanted **ustedes quisieron...** = you all wanted	**más dinero** = more money **escribir un libro** = to write a book **tener una fiesta** = to have a party **una buena nota** = a good grade **una beca** = a scholarship **llegar a tiempo** = arrive on time
QUERER = to want/ to wish *imperfect*	**generalmente** = generally **muchas veces** = many times **con frecuencia** = frequently	**yo quería...** = I used to want **usted quería...** = you used to want **ustedes querían...** = you all used to want	
TENER* = to have *preterite* *stem- uv*	**ayer por la tarde** = yesterday afternoon **esta mañana** = this morning **hace un año** = a year ago	**yo tuve...** = I had **usted tuvo...** = you had **ellos tuvieron...** = they had	**una taza de café** = a cup of coffee **un descanso** = a break **hambre** = hunger **sed** = thirst **calor** = heat (I was hot.) **frío** = cold (I was cold.) **prisa** = hurry (I was in a hurry.) **20 años** = 20 years (old)
TENER = to have *imperfect*	**usualmente** = usually **todos los días** = every day **mucho** = a lot	**yo tenía...** = I used to have **usted tenía...** = you used to have **ellos tenían...** = they used to have	

RESPUESTAS = ANSWERS

LECCIÓN 5
54 CINCUENTA Y CUATRO

1. mucha
2. poca
3. grandes
4. pequeña
5. blanco
6. negra
7. mayores
8. menor

SPANISH CHATBOOK ❷ © SPANISH CHAT COMPANY

RESPUESTAS = ANSWERS

LECCIÓN 5
55 CINCUENTA Y CINCO

LUGARES = PLACES

3. FALSE They drink mate which is a digestive tea and the Portuguese constructed the streets in 1680.

DÍAS FESTIVOS = HOLIDAYS

2. FALSE Labor Day is celebrated on May 1st in some countries and the date for Teacher's Day also varies to honor each of the National leaders in Education. Children's Day is October 10 in Chile, September 11 in Argentina, January 6 in Uruguay, April 30 in Paraguay and May 15 in Mexico. Many children look forward to receiving a toy or a gift on that day and the schools and many museums celebrate with special activities.

RESPUESTAS = ANSWERS

LECCIÓN 5
57 CINCUENTA Y SIETE

1. Ayer yo comí... = <u>Yesterday I ate...</u>
2. Yo comía mucho... = <u>I ate a lot...</u>
3. Antes de ayer ella comió.. = <u>The day before yesterday she ate...</u>
4. Él siempre vivía en... = <u>He always lived in...</u>
5. Hace muchos años yo viví en... = <u>Many years ago I lived in...</u>
6. En el pasado usted vivió con... = <u>In the past you lived with...</u>
7. Hace 10 años yo tuve... = <u>Ten years ago I had...</u>
8. Usualmente yo tenía... = <u>Usually I had...</u>
9. Generalmente ustedes tenían... = <u>Generally you all had...</u>
10. Yo todo el tiempo quería... = <u>All the time I wanted...</u>
11. La semana pasada yo quise... = <u>Last week I wanted...</u>
12. El otro día usted quiso... = <u>The other day you wanted...</u>

RESPUESTAS = ANSWERS

LECCIÓN 5
58 CINCUENTA Y OCHO

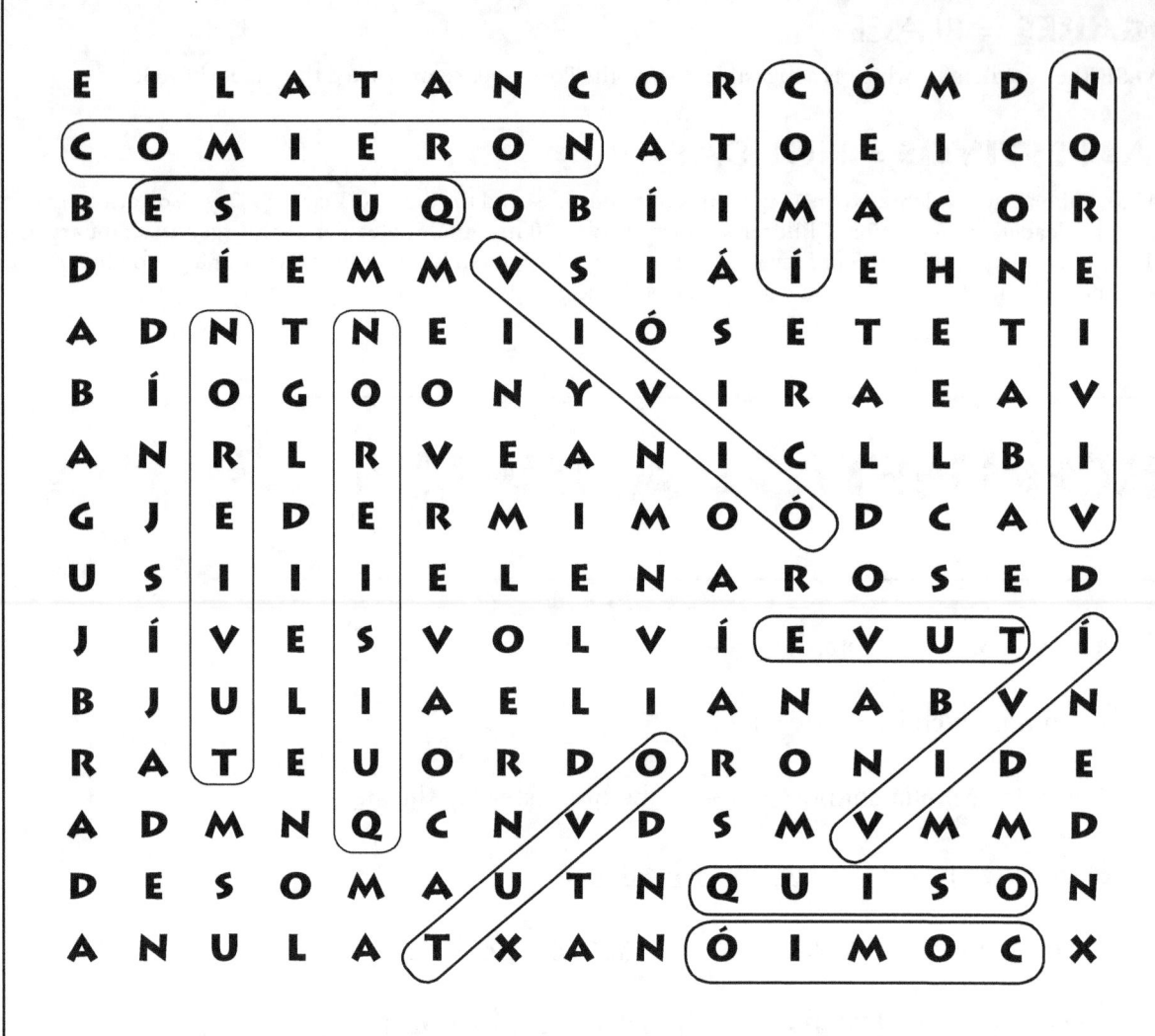

BUSCAPALABRAS = WORD SEARCH

(Note: these verbs are all in preterite past tense.)

1. he lived = **él vivió**
2. I had = **yo tuve**
3. they wanted = **ellos quisieron**
4. you all ate = **ustedes comieron**
5. she wanted = **ella quiso**
6. I lived = **yo viví**
7. you had = **usted tuvo**
8. I ate = **yo comí**
9. I wanted = **yo quise**
10. he ate = **él comió**
11. they had = **ellos tuvieron**
12. you all lived = **ustedes vivieron**

SPANISH CHATBOOK 2 © SPANISH CHAT COMPANY

RESPUESTAS = ANSWERS

LECCIÓN 6

IDEAS PARA LAS FRASES = IDEAS FOR SENTENCES

	USE THESE CLUES TO CHOOSE	CONJUGATIONS	POSSIBLE ENDINGS
IR* = to go *preterite* *memorize*	**antes de ayer** = the day before yesterday **la semana pasada** = last week **hace un año** = a year ago	(same as ser) **yo fui...** = I went **usted fue...** = you went **ustedes fueron...** = you all went	**a su última cita** = last date / appointment **al cine** = to the movie theater **a una isla en un crucero** = to an island on a cruise **la reunión** = the meeting
IR* = to go *imperfect* *memorize*	**a menudo** = often **todo el tiempo** = all the time **cada semana** = every week	**yo iba...** = I used to go **usted iba...** = you used to go **ustedes iban...** = you all used to go	**a comprar algo** = to buy something **al teatro** = to the theater **al dentista** = to the dentist **al museo** = to the museum **a la iglesia** = to the church
VER* = to see *preterite* *no accent*	**alguna vez** = some time **anoche** = last night **esta mañana** = this morning	**yo vi...** = I saw **usted vio...** = you saw **ellos vieron...** = they saw	**una película** = a movie **a alguien famoso** = someone famous **a un/a cantante** = a singer
VER = to see *imperfect*	**generalmente** = generally **cada día** = every day	**yo veía...** = I used to see **usted veía...** = you used to see **ellos veían...** = they used to see	**a mis (sus) hijos** = my children **algunos programas de televisión** = some T.V. shows **el partido de fútbol americano** = the football game
ESTAR* = to be (changing) *preterite* *stem -uv*	**una vez** = one time **a las ocho de la mañana** = at 8 a.m. **el otro día** = the other day	**yo estuve...** = I was **usted estuvo...** = you were **ustedes estuvieron...** = you all were	**emocionada(o)** = excited **enojada(o)** = mad **aburrida(o)** = bored **bien** = well **en España** = in Spain
ESTAR = to be (changing) *imperfect*	**a veces** = sometimes **muchas veces** = many times **usualmente** = usually	**yo estaba...** = I used to be **usted estaba...** = you used to be **ustedes estaban...** = you all used to be	**logrando (mis) sus metas** = achieving your goals **ganando becas** = winning scholarships **recibiendo buenas notas** = receiving good grades **aprendiendo español** = learning Spanish
SER* = to be (permanent) *preterite* *memorize*	**el último mes** = the last month **hace 2 días** = two days ago **en ese momento** = at that moment	(same as ir) **yo fui...** = I was **usted fue...** = you were **ellos fueron...** = they were	**un(a) estudiante de español en la secundaria** = a Spanish high school student **amigos de la infancia** = friends since childhood **ganadores del concurso** = contest winners
SER* = to be (permanent) *imperfect* *memorize*	**todos los días** = every day **mucho** = a lot **siempre** = always	**yo era...** = I used to be **usted era...** = you used to be **ellos eran...** = they used to be	**maestra de español** = Spanish teacher **invitados de honor** = guests of honor **de Argentina** = from Argentina

RESPUESTAS = ANSWERS

LECCIÓN 6

1. cerca
2. lejos
3. entre
4. con, durante
5. hasta

RESPUESTAS = ANSWERS

LECCIÓN 6
65 SESENTA Y CINCO

LUGARES = PLACES

1. FALSE For three reasons: First of all, in Puerto Rico, the "Castillo San Felipe del Morro" is named in honor of King Phillip II of Spain but he never resided there. Secondly, the Three Magi Kings are biblical characters that did not actually reside in the Cuban "Castillo de los Tres Reyes Magos del Morro." Finally, in Santo Domingo you can still visit the "Alcázar de Colón." Americas first castle and the residence of Don Diego, but it is not named a Morro.

DÍAS FESTIVOS = HOLIDAYS

3. FALSE Dictator Fidel died in 2017. Now his brother Raúl is the dictator. The Castros have been in power since 1959 with "elections" held every five years. Everyone is required to vote, but there is only one choice, "the leader of the communist party. candidate.

RESPUESTAS = ANSWERS

LECCIÓN 6
67 CUARENTA Y SIETE

1. Anoche yo vi... = <u>Last night I saw...</u>

2. Hace un mes ella vio... = <u>A month ago she saw...</u>

3. Mientras ella no veía.. = <u>While she did not see...</u>

4. Hace muchos años yo iba a... = <u>Many years ago I went to...</u>

5. De vez en cuando él iba a... = <u>Once in awhile...</u>

6. Ayer por la tarde usted fue... = <u>Yesterday afternoon you went...</u> (Note: fui could also mean "were")

7. En ese momento usted estuvo.. y entonces... = <u>In that moment I was...and then...</u>

8. Con frecuencia usted estaba... = <u>Frequently you were...</u>

9. A veces ustedes estaban.. = <u>Sometimes you all were...</u>

10. Todos los días yo era... = <u>Every day I was...</u>

11. Durante el año pasado yo fui... = <u>During the past year I was...</u> (Note: fui could also mean "went")

12. Hace un mes ellos fueron... = <u>A month ago they were...</u> (Note: fueron could also mean "went")

SPANISH CHATBOOK 2 © SPANISH CHAT COMPANY

RESPUESTAS = ANSWERS

LECCIÓN 6
68 SESENTA Y OCHO

1 you were (ser / preterite) =
usted _____ F U E

2 she went (ir / imperfect) =
ella _____ I B A

3 they saw (ver / imperfect) =
(all females) ellas _____ V E Í A N

4 I was (estar / preterite) =
yo _____ E S T U V E

5 he was (ser / imperfect) =
él _____ E R A
(Add an accent mark for the secret word below)

6 I was (estar / imperfect) =
él _____ E S T A B A

7 they were (estar / preterite) =
ellos _____ E S T U V I E R O N

8 I went (ir / preterite) =
yo _____ F U I

9 you all ate (comer / imperfect)
ustedes _____ C O M Í A N

10 you saw (ver / preterite) =
usted _____ V I O

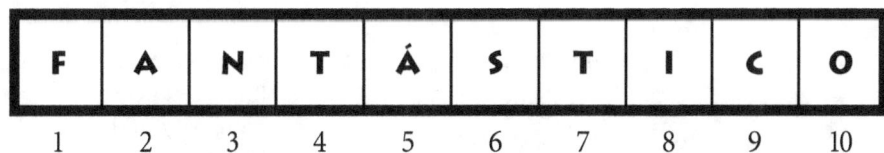

F A N T Á S T I C O
1 2 3 4 5 6 7 8 9 10

RESPUESTAS = ANSWERS

EXTRA GRAMMAR 77 — SETENTA Y SIETE

1. Inglés
2. bibliografía
3. ficción
4. dólares
5. puerta
6. periódico

RESPUESTAS = ANSWERS

EXTRA GRAMMAR 78 — SETENTA Y OCHO

1. A ella le gusta nadar.
2. Le gusta el libro.-formal (Te gusta el libro- informal)
3. A María y Bernardo les gusta leer.
4. A él le gusta pescar.
5. A ellos les gusta la pizza.
6. A mí me gustan los libros.
7. A mí me gusta viajar.
8. A nosotros nos gusta leer español.

RESPUESTAS = ANSWERS

EXTRA GRAMMAR 81 — OCHENTA Y UNO

1. acabo, acaba, acabamos, acaban
2. aprendo, aprende, aprendemos, aprenden
3. vivo, vive, vivimos, viven
4. hablo, habla
5. habla, hablan
6. habla, habla
7. leo, lee, lee,
8. leen, leemos,
9. lee, leer
10. asisto, asiste, asisten,
11. asistimos, asistir

RESPUESTAS = ANSWERS

EXTRA GRAMMAR 94 — NOVENTA Y CUATRO

1. fue
2. aprendimos
3. estudié
4. usé
5. escuchó
6. practicaban
7. hicieron
8. arreglaba
9. grabaron
10. hablaba
11. estuvo

Note: Numbers 6, 8, and 10 are imperfect because they happened with regularity in the past. 8 is imperfect because it happened cada semana = each week. Numbers 1-5, 7 and 9 are completed past actions, and therefore are conjugated in the preterite.

ÍNDICE  INDEX

SPANISH CHATBOOK 2

A

Absences, conversation / role play, 46
Accent marks, 76-77
Adjectives,
    Comparative, 54
    Demonstrative, 44
    Descriptive, 54
    Possessive, 34
Affirmative words, grammar, 24
Alphabet, intro before page 1
Alrededor del mundo game, 33
América Central, 35
América del Sur, 45, 55
Amigos, conversational role play, 16
Answer Key, after page 125
Appendix, 70-125
-ar past tense, 40-49, 86-94
-ar present tense, 10-19, 81-82
-ar irregular, 83-95
Argentina, 55
Around the world game, 33
Articles, grammar, 14
Audio CD track listing, 7
Author page, intro before page 1

B

Be, to (the verbs estar and ser),
    Past tense, 60-69
    Present tense, 30-39
Begin, to (the verb empezar),
    Past tense, 40-49
    Present tense, 10-19
Bingo = Lotería, 63
Bolivia, culture, 45
Book tour, intro before page 1
Boot verbs, irregular present, 83-85
Buscapalabras, word search, 28, 58

C

CD / Audio track listing, 7
Central America, 35
Charts,
    How to conjugate,
        12, 22, 32, 41, 42, 52, 62
    Past tense verbs, 41, 42, 52, 62, 66
    Present tense, 12, 22, 32, 39
    Preterite vs. Imperfect, 40, 49, 94
    Sentences, 12, 22, 32, 42, 52, 62
    Sixty present/past verbs, 114-125
    Twelve present tense verbs, 39
    Twelve preterite/imperfect, 66
Chile, 55
Choosing a Spanish name, 8
Colombia, culture, 45
Colors, 54
Comer, to eat
    Past tense, 50-59
    Present tense, 20-29
Comparative adjectives, 54
Con sus compañeros, page with your
    Colleagues, 11, 21, 31, 41, 51, 61
Concentration, matching game, 53
Conjugate verbs, charts & sentences,
    Past tense, 41, 42, 52, 62
    Present tense 12, 22, 32, 39
Conversational topics and role plays,
    Amigos = Friends, 16
    Client & Cashier, 36
    Family, 26
    Friends = Amigos, 16
    Gerente = Manager, 46
    Manager = Gerente, 46
    Tardiness, 16
    Trabajador = Worker, 46
    Travel, 36
    Two true/one false, 56
    Questions, 16, 26, 36, 46
    Sentence starters, 56
    Worker = Trabajador, 46
Continue learning, 10 ideas, 69

Countries, Spanish Speaking,
    15, 25, 35, 45, 55, 65
Costa Rica, culture, 35
Crossword puzzle/crucigrama, 18, 48
Crucigrama/crossword puzzle, 18, 48
Cuba, 65
Culture, 15, 25, 35, 45, 55, 65
    Argentina, 55
    Bolivia, 45
    Chile, 55
    Colombia, 45
    Costa Rica, 35
    Cuba, 65
    Dominican Republic, 65
    Ecuador, 45
    El Salvador, 35
    Equatorial Guinea, 65
    Guatemala, 35
    Guinea Equatorial, 65
    Honduras, 35
    La República Dominicana, 65
    Map, 9
    Mexico, 25
    Nicaragua, 35
    Panama, 35
    Paraguay, 55
    Peru, 45
    Puerto Rico, 65
    Spain, 15
    Uruguay, 55
    Venezuela, 45

D

Days of the week, intro before page 1
Demonstrative,
    Adjectives, 44
    Pronouns, 44
Descriptive adjectives, 54
Días Festivos = Holidays, 73-75
Dichos, 16, 26, 36, 46, 56, 66
Direct object pronouns, 79
Dominican Republic, 65

E

Eat, to (the verb comer),
　Past tense, 50-59
　Present tense, 20-29
Ecuador, culture, 45
El Salvador, culture, 35
Empezar, to begin/start,
　Past tense, 40-49
　Present tense, 10-19
Empieza aquí = start here page,
　10, 20, 30, 40, 50, 60
End, to (the verb terminar),
　Past tense, 40-49
　Present tense, 10-19
Equatorial Guinea, 65
-er past tense, 50-59, 86-95
-er present tense, 20-29, 81-85
Estar, to be, changing,
　Past tense, 60-69
　Present tense, 30-39
Estar vs. Ser, the verb to be, 30
Evaluation, final project rubric, 59
Exam,
　Final, 67
　Midterm oral, 39
Extra grammar, 76-94

F

Family,
　Conversational role play, 26
　List of members, 21
Feedback form, after page 69
Fill in the blank,
　Charts, 12, 22, 32, 42, 52, 62
　Secret word puzzles, 38, 68
　Translations, 17, 27, 47, 57, 67
Final Exam, 67
Final projects, proyectos finales,
　How to, requirements, 33
　Rubric for evaluation,
Finish, to (the verb terminar),
　Past tense, 40-49
　Present tense, 10-19
Flashcards, after page,
　12, 22, 32, 42, 52, 62
Flashcards of verb endings, 19
Food, list of, 50, 52
Friends, conversational role play, 16

G

Games, 13, 19, 23, 33, 43, 53, 63
　Alrededor del mundo, 33
　Around the world, 33
　Bingo = Lotería, 63
　Concentration, matching, 53
　Las Parejas, matching, 53
　Lotería = Bingo, 63
　Matching pairs, 53
　Take everything, 23
　Three-in-a-row/Tres En Raya, 13
　Toma Todo, 23
　Verb endings, 19
　Verbos y Dados/Verbs & Dice, 43
Gerente, conversational role play, 46
Glossary of vocabulary in the book,
　English = Spanish, 95-104
　Spanish = English, 105-113
Go, to (the verb ir),
　Past tense, 60-69
　Present tense, 30-39
Go-Go verbs song, 29
Grammar, 14, 24, 34, 44, 54, 64
　Accents, 76-77
　Adjectives,
　　Comparative, 54
　　Demonstrative, 44
　　Descriptive, 54
　　Possessive, 34
　Affirmative words, 24
　Articles, 14
　Comparative adjectives, 54
　Demonstrative,
　　Adjectives, 44
　　Pronouns, 44
　Descriptive adjectives, 54
　Direct object pronouns, 79
　Extra grammar / verbs, 76-94
　Gustar, (the verb to like), 78
　Imperfect vs. Preterite, 40, 49, 94
　Imperfect verbs, 40-69, 92-94
　Indirect object pronouns, 79
　Negative words, 24
　Nouns, 14
　Past tense verbs, 40-69, 86-94
　Positive words, 24
　Possessive,
　　Adjectives, 34
　　Pronouns, 34
　Prepositions, 64
　Present progressive, 80
　Present tense verbs, 10-39, 81-85
　Pronouns,
　　Demonstrative, 44
　　Possessive, 34
　Reflexive, 80
Guatemala, culture, 35
Guinea Equatorial, 65
Gustar, (the verb to like), 78

H

Hablar, to speak/talk,
　Past tense, 40-49
　Present tense, 10-19
Have, to (the verb tener),
　Past tense, 50-59
　Present tense, 20-29
Holidays, 15, 25, 35, 45, 55, 65, 73-75
Homework,
　Assigned pages, 17, 18, 27, 28, 37,
　　38, 47, 48, 57, 58, 67, 68
　Tracking page, intro before 1
Honduras, culture, 35
How to conjugate verbs,
　Past tense, 42, 52, 62
　Present tense 12, 22, 32

I

I know the verbs, yo sé los verbos,
　Charts, 12, 22, 32, 42, 52, 62
Ideas for sentences, with verb charts,
　Past tense, 42, 52, 62
　Present tense, 12, 22, 32
Ideas to continue learning, 69
Imperfect past tense,
　All 12 verbs in a chart, 66
　-ar verbs, 40-49, chart 42, 92-93
　-er verbs, 50-59, chart 52, 92-93
　Imperfect vs. Preterite, 40, 49, 94
　Irregular, 93
　Rule breakers, 60-69, chart 62
　Signal words, when to use, 49
Indirect object pronouns, 79
Introduction, book tour, intro before 1
Ir, to go,
　Past tense, 60-69
　Present tense, 30-39

J, K, L

Juegos, 13, 19, 23, 33, 43, 53, 63
La República Dominicana, 65
Las Parejas, matching game, 53
Like, to (the verb gustar), 78
Live, to (the verb vivir),
　Past tense, 50-59
　Present tense, 20-29
Lotería = Bingo, 63

M

Manager, conversational role play, 46
Map, Spanish Speaking Countries, 9
Matching,
　Activity, 37
　Game, 53
Mexico, culture, 25
Midterm exam, 39
Months of the year, before page 1

N

Name list and name tag, 8
Negative words, grammar, 24
Nosotros = We verbs, 78-93, 114-125
Nouns, grammar, 14
Number chart 1-1,000 on page 9

O / P

Oral midterm exam, after page 39
Order form, final page after index
Pairs, Parejas Matching game, 53
Panama, culture, 35
Paraguay, 55
Past tense (see preterite and/or imperfect)
Peru, culture, 45
Places, list of, 60
    To visit 15, 25, 35, 45, 55, 65
Positive phrases, 6
Positive words, grammar, 24
Possessive,
    Adjectives, 34
    Pronouns, 34
Prepositions, 64
Present progressive, 80
Present tense,
    All 12 verbs in a chart, 39
    Boot verbs, 83-84
    -ar verbs, 10-19, chart 12, 81-82
    -er verbs, 20-29, chart 22, 81-82
    Irregular verbs, 83-85
    Rule breaker verbs, 30-39, chart 32
Preterite past tense,
    All 12 verbs in a chart, 66
    -ar verbs, 40-49, chart 42, 86-94
    -er verbs, 50-59, chart 52, 86-94
    Irregular, 88-92, skateboard 91
    Preterite vs. Imperfect, 30, 49, 94
    Rule breakers, 60-69, chart 62
    Signal words, when to use, 49
Pronouns,
    Possessive, 34
    Demonstrative, 44
    Direct / indirect object, 79
Pronunciation of vowels, 10
Proyectos finales, final projects, 33
Puerto Rico, 65
Puzzle,
    Crossword = crucigrama, 18, 48
    Secret words, 38, 68
    Matching, 37
    Word search, 28, 58

Q / R

Querer, to want/wish,
    Past tense, 50-59
    Present tense, 20-29
Questions, role play, 16, 26, 36, 46
Recipes = Recetas, 70-72
Reflexive, 80
Role plays, conversational,
    16, 26, 36, 46, 56, 66
Rubric, final project evaluation, 59
Rule breaker verbs,
    Past tense, 60-69
    Present tense, 30-39

S

Secret word puzzles, 38, 68
See, to (the verb ver),
    Past tense, 60-69
    Present tense, 30-39
Sentence & conversational starters, 56
Ser, to be, permanent
    Past tense, 60-69
    Present tense, 30-39
Ser vs. Estar, 30
Signal words, preterite/imperfect, 49
Skateboard verbs, irregular preterite, 91
Song, Go-Go verbs, 29
South America, 45, 55
Spain, culture, 15
Spanish Speaking countries, map, 9
    Culture, 15, 25, 35, 45, 55, 65
Speak, to (the verb hablar),
    Past tense, 40-49
    Present tense, 10-19
Start here, empieza aquí page,
    10, 20, 30, 40, 50, 60
Start, to (the verb empezar),
    Past tense, 40-49
    Present tense, 10-19
Student guide & helpful hints, 4

T

Take everything game, 23
Table of contents, 1-3
Table of 60 verbs in present/past, 114-125
Talk, to (the verb hablar),
    Past tense, 40-49
    Present tense, 10-19
Tardiness, conversational role play, 16
Tarea, homework, 17, 18, 27, 28, 37, 38, 47,
    48, 57, 58, 67, 68
Teacher guide & helpful hints, 5
Ten ideas to continue learning, 69
Tener, to have,
    Past tense, 50-59
    Present tense, 20-29
Terminar, to finish/end,
    Past tense, 40-49
    Present tense, 10-19
Thank you page, after subject index
Three-in-a-row, Tres en Raya game, 13
Time, 11
Toma Todo game, 23
Trabajar, to work,
    Past tense, 40-49
    Present tense, 10-19
Trabajador, conversational role play, 46
Translation exercises, 17, 27, 47, 57, 67
Travel,
    Conversational role play, 16
    Cultural info, 15, 25, 35, 45, 55, 65
Tourist game, 20
Tres En Raya game Three-in-a-row, 13
Tú = informal you verbs, 78-93, 114-125
Tú vs. usted, 4, 81

U, V

Uruguay, 55
Venezuela, culture, 45
Ver, to see,
    Past tense, 60-69
    Present tense, 30-39
Verbs
    -ar,
        Past tense, 40-49, chart 42
        Present tense, 10-19, chart 12
    Conjugation chart, 12, 22, 32, 42, 52, 62
    -er,
        Past tense, 50-59, chart 52
        Present tense, 20-29, chart 22
    Games,
        Verb endings, 19
        Verbs and Dice, 43
    Go-Go, with song, 29
    Irregular
        Imperfect, 93
        Past tense, 88-93
        Present, Boot, 83-85, Go-Go, 29
        Preterite, 88-92, skateboard 91
    Past, 40-69, chart of all, 66, 86-92, 94
    Present tense, 10-39, 81-85
    Present progressive, 80
    Preterite tense, 40-69, 86-92, 94
    Reflexive, 80
    Rule breaker verbs,
        Past tense, 60-69, chart 62
        Present, 30-39, charts 32 & 39
    Verbs and Dice game, 43
Vivir, to live,
    Past tense, 50-59
    Present tense, 20-29
Vocabulary in the book, Glossary, 95-113
Vosotros, Ya'll verb forms, 78-93, 114-125
Vowels, pronunciation, 10

W, X, Y, Z

Want, to (the verb querer),
    Past tense, 50-59
    Present tense, 20-29
Weather, intro before page 1
When to use preterite / imperfect, 30, 49
With your colleagues, 11, 21, 31, 41, 51, 61
Word search, 28, 58
Words that signal preterite/imperfect, 49
Work, to (the verb trabajar),
    Past tense, 40-49
    Present tense, 10-19
Worker, conversational role play, 46
Yo sé los verbos, 12, 22, 32, 42, 52, 62

Gracias = Thank You

The *Spanish Chatbook 2* is dedicated to the many people around the world that are working very hard to support their families and learn another language. I hope to build bridges through communication and connect our global society. Now you will be able to speak another language and get to know a new "amigo" or "amiga." Gracias y saludos to my family and friends, son Jaden, daughter Elena, husband Brad, my students and future travelers everywhere. Thanks to Indira Engel, Gonzalo Baron, Vieva McClure, Luisa Olson, Curtis Grubb, Laura Mattuch and Designer Wendy Biernbaum. An extra thanks to my parents and grandparents who have been amazing role models for my husband and I, and have taken care of our children while I worked on the book. Thank you for helping me make my dreams become realities. To my readers and Spanish students, thank you for taking your time and putting in the effort to learn Spanish. Feel free to visit our Web site SpanishChatCompany.com to give us feedback, or ask questions. If you have any suggestions or changes for a future edition, just let us know. I would love to hear testimonials of how this *Spanish Chatbook 2* has helped you. Keep practicing and keep smiling. Your journey has just begun.
¡Buen Viaje! = Enjoy the adventure!

Do you need anything else? = ¿Necesita algo más?

Want to order more books for coworkers, friends, or your entire company?
Here is how: Order online at SpanishChatCompany.com or fill out this form and mail it to Spanish Chat Company.

Name _____

Address _____

City, State, Zip _____

Phone/email _____

Spanish Chat Company   Phone: (402) 398-1384   (7:00 a.m. to 7:00 p.m. CST)
PO Box 45934   Fax: (402) 398-1384
Omaha, NE 68145   E-mail: SpanishChatCompany@gmail.com
     Order online at SpanishChatCompany.com

ITEM	BOOK	CD	BOTH
Spanish Chatbook	$19.95 ☐	$14.95 ☐	$34.90 ☐
Spanish Chatbook 2	$29.95 ☐	$14.95 ☐	$44.90 ☐
Culinary Spanish Chatbook	$29.95 ☐	$14.95 ☐	$44.90 ☐
Business Spanish Chatbook	$29.95 ☐	$14.95 ☐	$44.90 ☐
Elementary Spanish Chatbook	$29.95 ☐	$19.95 ☐	$49.90 ☐

ITEM	DVD
Spanish Chatshow: ¡Cocínalo! = Cook It!	$19.95 ☐
Spanish Chatshow: ¡Repítelo! = Repeat It!	$19.95 ☐

ITEM	CD
Un Tiempo Para Sanar = A Time to Heal (Education, training and support for cancer survivors in Spanish)	$19.95 ☐

Subtotal   + $ _____

Sales Tax (Nebraska residents add 7% sales tax)   + $ _____

Shipping & Handling ($6 per item for ground shipping within the United States)   + $ _____

Total (Make checks payable to Spanish Chat Company) $ _____

www.ingramcontent.com/pod-product-compliance
Lightning Source LLC
Chambersburg PA
CBHW081216230426
43666CB00015B/2757